D0877143

RECONSTRUCTING
EDUCATIONAL PSYCHOLOGY

RECONSTRUCTING EDUCATIONAL PSYCHOLOGY

EDITED BY BILL GILLHAM

CROOM HELM LONDON

© 1978 Foreword Jack Tizard; Ch. 1 Bill Gillham; Ch. 2 Tony Dessent;
Ch. 3 Tony Dessent; Ch. 4 Michael Roe; Ch. 5 David Hargreaves; Ch. 6
Bill Gillham; Ch. 7 David Loxley; Ch. 8 Robert Burden; Ch. 9 Frank Carter;
Ch. 10 Andrew Sutton; Ch. 11 Gervase Leyden

Croom Helm Ltd, 2-10 St John's Road, London SW11

British Library Cataloguing in Publication Data

Reconstructing educational psychology.
　　1. School psychologists – Great Britain
　　I. Gillham, William Edwin Charles
　　371.7'1　　　LB3013.6

　　ISBN 0-85664-631-8
　　ISBN 0-85664-667-9 Pbk

Printed and bound in Great Britain by
Billing & Sons Limited, Guildford, London and Worcester

CONTENTS

PREFATORY NOTE

This book makes no pretensions to being 'radical' except in the sense of reflecting the radical changes that are taking place in the profession of educational psychology as a whole. In reading it educational psychologists will recognise their own ideas and their own developments in practice: the contributors are articulating shared responses to common experience. It was this essential unity of the character of change that led the editor to propose the work in the first place. As Gervase Leyden comments in the final chapter ' . . . although these developments are not centrally orchestrated they are forming a recognisable movement'. In other words the unity is not a forced, or even a negotiated, one; there are differences, but these are less impressive than the overall coherence of views — which augurs well for the process of reconstruction.

In writing their chapters contributors have been free to make a personal statement, which means that their views do not necessarily reflect those of their employing authorities.

Much of the detailed editing was carried out by my wife, Judith: all contributions have been improved as a result of her work; and the smooth production of the book was greatly helped by Margaret Grainger's impeccable typescript.

B.G.

FOREWORD

The Summerfield Report on *Psychologists in Education Services* (1968),
which was intended to usher in a new era in educational psychology,
seems in retrospect to have marked the end of an old one. Certainly,
during the last ten years there has been, among educational psychologists, an increasing questioning of their role, and of the job descriptions
spelled out so painstakingly in Summerfield. There are three main
sources of dissatisfaction with this. First, waiting lists. How will it ever
be possible for psychologists, with recommended case loads four times
as large as those of general practitioners, to end the nightmare of the
waiting lists which force them to run ever faster in order to stay in the
same place? Secondly disillusionment both with diagnosis and with
treatment; as David Loxley puts it: Was Burt's client 'the backward
child' or 'the young delinquent' or was it in fact the London County
Council? Thirdly, and as a consequence, educational psychologists are
coming to see their clients as being the classes and the schools and the
community, rather than the individual, troubled children who have been
traditionally referred to them for diagnosis and disposal.

This book is concerned with these issues. It consists of essays by
serious and well informed psychologists all of whom are trying to tackle
in new ways the intractable problems that confront them in their own
practice.

The book contains a good deal that I don't myself agree with — and
this is hardly surprising since the authors don't espouse a monolithic
party line but disagree among themselves too, on important points. But
even where they find themselves of one mind, I can't always go along
with them. Thus they don't, I think, take sufficient account of the
serious criticisms that have been made of the school of Thomas Szasz,
and of labelling theory; and they give too much weight in my view to
Shepherd *et al.*'s destructive criticisms of child guidance and ignore the
points made for example in Rutter's critical notice of this important
study (*J. Child Psychol. Psychiat. 13* (1972), 219-22). Of course these
and other, related issues will continue to be debated; and it is valuable
to have an extended presentation of a case, *especially* if it isn't one that
you necessarily accept.

However for me the most interesting and important parts of this
book were those in which the writers describe what they actually do.

The accounts are most informative and heartening. Clearly there are many new and different things going on: and all who are concerned with educational psychology will find a good deal here that is new to them, and be led to think again about how educational psychology can be reconstructed.

Jack Tizard

Professor of Child Development
Thomas Coram Research Unit
University of London Institute of Education

1 DIRECTIONS OF CHANGE*

Bill Gillham

Few professions can have gone through such a radical change in basic practices and ideas as have educational psychologists during the past decade. Indeed, during the past two or three years change has been proceeding at an almost exponential rate so that the professional scene has been looking somewhat confused. It has, I suggest, been the apparent confusion of a profession changing course, and only recently has it been possible to see in what direction it is now pointed as well as some of the snags and difficulties that lie ahead. One thing is clear: that the main changes are coming about because of the reworking and rethinking of educational psychologists who have become grossly dissatisfied with traditional practice. Certainly recent legislative and administrative changes have had an effect on the nature of psychologists' work: these changes are well summarised by Wright (1976); but new responsibilities do not have to be assumed in traditional ways. What is most striking about educational psychologists as a group is that, like women, they have become increasingly intolerant of the burden of traditional expectations. Instead of allowing themselves to continue to be formed by established social expectancies (to whose formation they have in the past contributed), they are actively redefining their role. This is not to deny the effects of changed circumstances that are making role changes possible. These changes are many and some of them are fairly general.

Educational psychologists are part of a wider group who have taken a basic first degree course in psychology (although not all educational psychologists have, in fact, done this). In most universities this basic course still mainly aims to provide a grounding in experimental psychology and research methods: in so far as it can be said to have a career orientation it is in the direction of becoming a research worker in experimental psychology; there are relatively few such posts which means that, for most professional psychologists, there is no detailed carry over of content and method into their working lives. For the most part they cannot be 'applied' psychologists because much of the

---

*This chapter is based on a paper given at the DES course 'Psychological Services and the Schools' held at Sheffield Polytechnic in September 1977.

11

psychology they have learnt is irrelevant to the problems they are faced
with, or else incapable of application. This poses real difficulties for the
practitioner psychologist who has to develop ways of coping and some
of these may be rather makeshift: of this he has usually been somewhat
ashamed and, for his pains, looked down on by the university departments who failed to equip him adequately in the first place, e.g. the
head of a psychology department quoted in the Summerfield Report
(DES, 1968) who suggested that educational psychologists were
typically seen as 'intuitionists and ex-teachers with green fingers'. Such
a comment sums up a fairly general attitude in the sixties. The phenomenon of the seventies has been the greatly improved confidence and
status of practitioner psychology in contrast to academic psychology in
general, and experimental psychology in particular. It would not be
overly dramatic to say that academic psychology seems to have lost its
nerve, and is busy putting on an applied face to conceal its uncertainties.
It is a truly amazing change to those who have lived through it.

The areas of academic psychology which are currently the most
popular are those with most relevance to everyday life — social,
developmental and phenomenological psychology. It was precisely
these aspects of the subject which the 'hard science' psychology of the
early sixties neglected: the status activities of that time were natural
science style experimental psychology and the computer simulation of
psychological processes. In particular much was hoped for the latter
which were going to create 'models of man' and even to be 'the first
true saints' — because passionless. But as Neisser (1976) has recently
reminded us it is passion and purpose, social influence and *growth* that
are the distinctive features of human psychology.

The high status areas in the academic psychology of the early sixties
suffered a severe reverse in their fortunes within the same decade. It
was not just that such activities became less valued but that they failed
within their own terms. The basic 'objective' methodology of experimental psychology proved to have its own social psychology, to be
enormously vulnerable to the expectations of the experimenter and his
subjects (Rosenthal, 1966), as well as incapable of resolving theoretical
questions formulated in its own terms (Howarth, 1975). Human
psychology proved disconcertingly difficult to simulate even in the
area of so-called 'logical' processes and it became clear that the principles of organisation and discrimination were very different in man and
machine. Attempts to simulate language production resulted in sen-
tences that read like ambiguous telegrams. Great labours produced
small results. A research programme at the University of Edinburgh

attempted to simulate visual processes: at the end of three years and £30,000 the computer could tell a cup from a saucer; and it took eight minutes to do it.* A lot of expectations collapsed and at a time when the attitude in society at large towards academic research was distinctly critical. By the early seventies the new priorities were clear: the man with something to offer and something to say was the practitioner, or at least the applied psychologist; the general concern was to get in on the act.

If I appear to labour this point it is because I see it as an important one. Educational psychologists are human beings too: if they perceive themselves as having greater value and status that increases their confidence — and their ability to change. A defensive stance is also an inflexible one: it requires self-confidence to be self-questioning.

Of course, the educational psychologist's reappraisal, like the self-doubts of the academic psychologist, does not arise from purely internal professional concerns. To some extent they both arise out of a heightened awareness of economic and moral responsibility for the positions we occupy, the activities we engage in — and the comfortable salaries we draw: it is the age of accountability. In this process cost-effectiveness ranks high. Even allowing for the tough-mindedness induced by the economic recession of recent years it is clear that we cannot afford further expansion of medical and social services *as they are at present constituted*. An expansion policy based on what Andrew Sutton (1976) calls 'more of the same' is not going to be tolerated except in cases of proven effectiveness (see Chapter 10). The consequences of the expansion during the economic boom of the sixties are well summarised by Midwinter (1977):

Between 1961 and 1974 employment of full and part-time workers by local authorities rose by 54%, by central government 9% . . . Many of the extra jobs have gone to administrators instead of to the people who deal with patients or children or clients. Between 1965 and 1973 the administrative staff in the NHS hospitals increased by 51% while the number of beds occupied fell away. In just four years NHS administrative and clerical staff grew by 31% and medical staff by only 19.7%. The same kind of thing has been happening in education. Only half of the 1,453,000 people employed by local author-

---

*I am grateful to Professor Richard Gregory for permission to quote this self-mocking remark made at the inaugural meeting of the BPS Developmental Psychology Section in October 1972; Professor Gregory adds that the computer could recognise the cup from any angle — provided that the handle was in view.

ities in education are actually teachers. Over the years employment of this kind has been deliberately extended, rather than in productive capacity industries, because there was little or no need for heavy capital investment — it has been a politico-economic rather than a social series of decisions.

He continues:

I gaze half-benignly on cuts in public expenditure. If those cuts can mean . . . the properly directed deprofessionalisation and deinstitutionalisation of our public services and the controlled mobilisation of community resources, then I am convinced the overall quality of services would be improved. Gone is the time when management or labour can claim that a service *automatically* deteriorates if expenditure is reduced.

The paper from which these quotations are taken was given in London in October 1976; since then I think you could add a few turns to the screw. In the same paper Midwinter relates the costly proliferation of the 'helping' services to the process of professionalisation. He suggests that, just about without exception, all groups ' have slavishly adhered to the historic fate mapped out for professions. They have become bureaucratised, defensive about manning and function, haunted by false fears of "dilution", jittery about evaluation and open accountability, jargon-plagued, status-conscious, and sheltering, in a pother of insecurity, behind a barricade of mystiques.'

The clear implication is that there is no security in such defensiveness. The encouraging thing about educational psychology is that the profession seems to be moving into a position of open accountability — linked to a more precise definition of the client.

Educational psychologists have, in the past, experienced some confusion as to just who their client is; it has sometimes seemed that the psychologist must be all things to all men. The present trend seems to be to make a distinction between the primary client, the child, and the secondary clients, who include the employing authority. The problem is to maintain this priority and I think this relates to the now more commonly expressed feeling amongst psychologists that, for professional purposes, they should be independent of education authorities. It is simple to affirm that co-operation with parents, teachers, educational administrators and the like, must be conditional on the child's interests being served. Most of the time there is an effective identity of interest, but at times it is necessary for a child's advocate to intervene in a process that is working against his client: it may be something as subtle as the process of defining a child as 'maladjusted' or 'subnormal' which, with no sinister intention, is none the less happening in a sinister fashion (see Chapter 5); or it may be something as flagrant as a 'best fit' school placement which is the best fit for the local authority but not for the child. These are not always easy things to resist but it is my strong impression that educational psychologists are increasingly willing to tackle this kind of issue.

This essentially moral attitude goes along with a greater willingness to work with parents and teachers as a colleague rather than as a consultant — an attitude which recognises the primary importance of those adults who have most to do with a child, and the primary effectiveness of altering what happens *between* an adult and a child — be it changes in teaching method, handling or attitude — to achieve changes for the child. It also recognises the absurdity of the psychologist as the man with the magic gift with children — he probably hasn't got it and if he has he's not around most of the time to use it. It puts a premium on talking language, ideas and techniques that people can use, because if they can't it is unlikely that anything effective can be done.

In common with many other professions, including medicine, educational psychologists have become increasingly aware of the disadvantages of conspicuous professionalisation: it is a particular handicap for the psychologist. By the very nature of their trade educational psychologists can only really be effective through other people; which means that any 'turn-offs' in the form of status trappings and professional mystiques actually render them less effective — even if it does make them look more like members of traditional, established professions. Despite some hesitation in the recent past it seems that educational psychologists have the opportunity — and the inclination — to avoid the dread fate mapped out by Eric Midwinter and to reprofessionalise in a way which avoids the main dangers of professionalism. Accountability is at the heart of it.

In a sense both economic and moral accountability are one: they both demand that the psychologist should be able to *do* something; even moral attitudes are empty if nothing happens. Certainly a barrage of statistics about work-loads and increasing areas of responsibility cuts no ice. Hawks' (1971) comment about clinical psychologists is relevant here: 'Too often clinical psychologists offer as justification of what they

are doing, the fact that they are over-worked doing it; less often can it be
claimed that what they are doing is known to have some beneficial effect.'

This dilemma has increasingly preoccupied educational psychologists
during the past two or three years and the desire for greater effectiveness has led to major changes in role definition. The main directions of
change seem to be these:

- decreasing emphasis on individual work with children individually
  referred;
- increasing emphasis on indirect methods of helping children's
  learning problems and problems of social adjustment — through
  the organisation, policy and structure of schools, through the
  attitudes and behaviour of adults towards children;
- increasing emphasis on preventive work through educational
  screening and courses for parents and teachers — encouraging them
  to carry out their own assessment and remediation procedures.

Very broadly speaking educational psychologists are becoming less clinical
and more educational which means there are problems of adjustment to
other professional groups, such as educational advisers, who sometimes
feel that psychologists are invading their territory by taking an interest in
school organisation and curriculum reform, instead of confining their
attention to individual 'cases'. There can be no more simple index of the
drift of change than these demarcation disputes: ten years ago the role conflict would have been with medical officers and child psychiatrists.

But the brake on progress is not such territorial disputes, which are
really of a minor character, but the weight of child guidance traditions
which psychologists still trail behind them (see Chapters 2 and 11).
Nearly half a century of child guidance has not proved easy to throw
off. In a very real sense the story of child guidance is a kind of tragedy.
I know of nothing that conveys this more clearly than the article by
Olive Sampson published in the mid-seventies and entitled 'A dream
that is dying?', in which she wrote about the personal and professional
sacrifices of those who supported child guidance in its early days. It was
an investment in something that we can now see as bound to fail: few
of us would disagree with Tizard's (1973) judgement of child guidance
as 'wrongly conceived'. It was not just that children who were seen by
the child guidance team derived no more enduring benefit than those who
were not, or who declined treatment; nor that it only saw a minority of
children with problems and excluded some categories altogether. Its
failure was even more basic than that. Writing in 1972 Kingsley
Whitmore observed: 'The child guidance service is often thought of as a

preventive service and it was the dream of the pioneer clinics that they would reduce the incidence of mental disorder in children. This dream has not really come true, for children only make contact with the service when a problem has arisen that their parents and/or teachers cannot manage.' Child guidance failed at many levels but the foundation of its failure was the way in which it recruited its clients: ineffectual individual treatment was merely a corollary of this.

With increasing momentum during the past ten years, and particularly since local government reorganisation in 1974, school psychological services have been abstracting themselves physically and administratively from child guidance. But they have tended to take many of the old practices with them, including the most basic one − the individual crisis-driven referral which usually goes to that all-embracing practitioner, the waiting list, whose therapeutic cure is time.

When over half of the School Psychological Services in England and Wales had only one educational psychologist and only 15 per cent had more than four (Summerfield Report, op. cit.), it seemed sensible to ascribe the long lists of children waiting to be seen to chronic undermanning. Yet ten years after Summerfield, services that have trebled or quadrupled in size are finding themselves in an identical situation. The obvious lesson is that you cannot beat the open-ended waiting list, even if it were worthwhile doing so. It is possible, by sprinting from school to school (and giving what Topping (1977) describes as 'emergency reading and intelligence tests'), to keep the vanishing tail of the waiting list in sight, even if forever out of reach. But the rapid processing of referrals does mean that the psychologist usually has little time for more than the reflex activity of 'testing'.

Even where the waiting list phenomenon is being subverted or brought under control, the social obligation to test is proving difficult to avoid. I have a suspicion that many of the individual intelligence tests given by psychologists these days are given because they cannot avoid doing them: it is difficult to battle against tacit (or explicit) expectations. You cannot give a lecture on mental testing theory to every co-professional who asks for a report. Teachers, social workers, doctors, administrators know what a psychological report is, they've been seeing them for years − it is a test report with the results in a little box at the top: they must be rather bewildered by the psychologist's change of attitude.

Routine testing is, for the psychologist, the corollary of the traditional individual referral, the expected response. To borrow from George Orwell's parable: you are known as the man with the gun and you have to shoot the rogue elephant that has been found for you; your feelings of futility, your sense that this is not your decision, is of no avail. Other people locate the problems for you and require you to deal with them in the way they have come to expect. Like Orwell's experience as a colonial administrator, the educational psychologist's role discomfort is due to the unself-critical, confident performance of those who have gone before him or, more ironical still, his own earlier days. The trap of testing expectations is not just that it involves him in doing things he may doubt the meaning or use of, but also that it shackles him to individual tests that are usually 'restricted' and can only be given by a qualified educational psychologist: it is part of the professional fate outlined by Eric Midwinter.

The individual referral and the individual test have as their inevitable consequence that most impossible (but persistent) expectation, the individual cure. It is, of course, an expectation originally created by a remote clinic and mysterious treatments. Two things, I suggest, have saved the school psychologist from conspicuous and ignominious failure in this respect, both of which cast an interesting light on the credulity and superstition of head-teachers. One is the rarity of the psychologist's visits which, to the hopeful, invest his most ordinary comments and actions with special significance; the other is that most children get over their difficulties anyway and often soon enough after the psychologist's visit for him to get the credit. We all have our own dramatic stories to tell on this theme — the behaviour problems that disappeared after the child had been given two sub-tests of the WISC; the enuresis that was apparently cured by taking a developmental history from the child's mother. Of course this sort of fraud is no more satisfying (although less painful) than abject and conspicuous impotence, but it does serve to confuse the picture.

All the signs are that we know what we have to do, even if there are problems in implementation. Tizard (1976) has this to say: 'It seems to me . . . that there is a need to sort ourselves out, to make it clear what we can and cannot do, to concentrate our resources on what is likely to be effective. If we do not do this we will be likely to suffer the fate that has overtaken social workers — become a crisis-driven profession obliged to tackle innumerable problems which we have no hope of alleviating.'

We surely know that the psychological problems of children are infinite: we could spend our professional lives whirling through space, never touching down.

Most children's difficulties are transitory, this being particularly true of emotional problems and many kinds of social difficulties. Cummings, an educational psychologist working in Leicester and later in Hampshire demonstrated this very clearly over thirty years ago (Cummings, 1944, 1946). Shepherd, Oppenheim and Mitchell (1971) in their more recent longitudinal study in Buckinghamshire showed that of 400 children originally assessed as 'deviant' on the basis of behavioural signs, 50 per cent, four years later were 'deviance' free and a further 25 per cent markedly improved — the same improvement rate as for those children who had attended child guidance clinics. Change appeared to be related to broad changes in children's circumstances — which indicates both the extent of behavioural determinants and the limits of intervention (see Chapter 7).

Apart from mental retardation and educational failure the most enduring problems presented by children are aggressive and anti-social behaviours which persist across different relationships and different situations: there are more contexts in which to maintain them. Contrary to one of the key assumptions of child guidance this is also the group with the worst long-term outcome in 'mental health' terms. Central to the philosophy of child guidance was the belief (derived from psycho-analytic theory) that emotional problems in childhood, unless treated, would lead to neurotic disorders in adult life. The anxious and withdrawn child, it was thought, should be the focus of concern. One particularly influential piece of research was that of Wickman (1928) who showed that teachers worked on different assumptions and were more inclined to regard outwardly difficult children as problems — presumably because of their lack of child-centredness and desire for a quiet life. Part of the evangelism of the mental health movement in the 1920s, from which child guidance is mainly derived, was to secure recognition of the alleged seriousness of the less conspicuous emotional problems.

Whilst the motives of the teachers in Wickman's study may not have been of the disinterested kind, more recent longitudinal research suggests that their concern was rightly placed. Robins (1966) in her study *Deviant Children Grown Up* was able to follow up groups of people who as children had been assessed, broadly, as having 'neurotic' as against 'sociopathic' difficulties in childhood; she compared them with a group who had not been identified as presenting such difficulties at the same age. Her findings were interesting in that in adult life the 'neurotic' group was virtually indistinguishable, in terms of current difficulties, from the 'normal' group; but the group that had exhibited aggressive and anti-social behaviour in childhood was markedly different in adult life in terms of all kinds of psychological problems. Robins subsequently brought together a wide range of studies which pointed in the

same direction (Robins, 1970, 1972). In other words it would seem
that Wickman's teachers (motives apart) were right.

My purpose in citing this research is not to suggest that psychologists
should not concern themselves with the anxious and withdrawn child
or any other, probably transitory, problems that cause much current
unhappiness, but that the criterion for the psychologist's effectiveness
should relate mainly to his ability to modify or ameliorate those
difficulties which are likely to be most enduring. I have started off with
the area of emotional and social problems because it is the one where
matters are most confused.

We know that cognitive characteristics are more stable, across time
and situation, than emotional and social behaviours (Mischel, 1968).
The child who is a behaviour problem at school is not particularly
likely to be so at home (and vice versa), but the child who has difficulty
in reading at school is almost certainly like that at home as well.
Educational psychologists have always concerned themselves with
problems of mental retardation and basic educational failure. In the
past, however, the tendency has been for their investigation to be
focused on within-the-child diagnosis: to quote Michael Roe —
'tiny deficits in sequencing or short term memory are made to
explain huge reading deficits' (Chapter 4). All this is changing,
partly because of an awareness of the bogus or circular nature of
'explanations' offered by 'intelligence' or 'ability' tests (see Chapter
6) and partly because of doubts about the ascertainment function
(of special educational need) and the uncertain benefits of special
education as a form of institutional provision (see Chapter 11).
A recommendation as to placement and a broad indication of need is
no longer seen as adequate; the great weakness of the recently
established — but non-statutory — SE procedure (DES,Circular 2/75) is
that it does not really go any further than this.

In terms of professional practice the shift in emphasis is quite
distinct: the psychologist's appraisal of a child and his difficulties is now
much more in terms of the means of achieving change, rather than
burrowing into the past or into the psyche in pursuit of causes and
explanations. Speculations about the causes of my wretched state, no
matter how perceptive and insightful, do not necessarily tell me anything about how to change it. The heart of educational psychology must
be the theory and technology of change and this takes the psychologist a
long way from being a mere clinician. It means, to use Frank Carter's phrase,
different 'levels of operation — the level of the individual, of the group
or institution, and the wider context of the community and local

government (see Chapter 9). It is at these last two levels that the psychologist, by default of the past, is changing most conspicuously. In his concern to help the individual child he is becoming less individualist. As educational psychologists have become more genuinely school and community psychologists so learning and behaviour problems have increasingly come to be seen as problems between adults and children within the context of the school or home. One of the bonuses of becoming less clinical is that psychologists are enabled to think in terms of psychological (and therefore, social) rather than medical constructs (see Chapter 4).

The force of our experience has moved us irresistibly in this direction and is paralleled by more formal evidence. Tizard (op. cit.) referring to the work of Michael Power and his colleagues, comments that the investigation of individuals 'throws no light at all on the . . . question of why average delinquency rates in secondary modern schools in East London should vary from 6 per 1,000 in one to 77 per 1,000 in another, or why two schools which are apparently matched closely for "external characteristics" should have average annual first court appearances of 14 and 59 over a ten-year period (Power, Benn and Morris, 1972)'. With the individual child in mind (but not 'treating' the individual) the psychologist's contribution may be at the level of improving the nature of pastoral care or remedial provision within a school, encouraging the development of a PTA, or supporting parents' attempts to establish a playgroup; we could all think of some more politically contentious things as well. There can be few educational psychologists who are not now working in this way, to some extent at least. Such an exposed position makes considerable personal demands on the psychologist and it is easy to see why some prefer to retreat to the more protected territory of a clinic. This is not to say that there is never a need for a clinical perspective particularly in the case of very exceptional children with highly transferable problems; what I am suggesting is that it is not relevant to the problems of most children and is basically different from the main work of being an educational psychologist.

Operating at the level of the institution is essentially a preventive stance, true to the child guidance ideal but not the practice. So also is working with groups of teachers or parents on change-orientated topics like behaviour modification, the teaching of reading, language development, and the construction of criterion- or content-referenced assessment schedules linked to remediation programmes. Both the institutional and the group (or 'project') approaches (see Chapters 7 and 8) reflect a desire to help children indirectly through influencing what happens to them, the quality of their daily experience — which is more likely to determine change than once a week treatment or remediation sessions. If the educational psychologist is increasingly taking such a mediational role it does not imply that investigating an individual child's difficulties is not seen as important: it does imply that a little tampering with the child and his immediate circumstances may be to no avail. Individual assessment does not necessarily entail action at the individual level, particularly when one child's difficulties can be seen as common to many others in the same circumstances. A particular child's problems have an unanswerable validity and can often crystallise the need for more general action. It is worth noting that important legislation for children, e.g. the 1948 Children's and Young Persons' Act, has often been precipitated by public concern about an individual case (Pinchbeck and Hewitt, 1973). The educational psychologist who takes his focus altogether off the individual child is heading for the woolly land occupied by educational sociologists.

One of the dangers of our present position is that our awareness of the inadequacies of our traditional wares may lead us to restock too rapidly with new goods of inferior quality — as is evident, for example, in the current proliferation of makeshift screening procedures (see Chapter 6). It is too easy to dismiss criticism of innovation as the reflex responses of reactionaries: if there are psychologically dubious reasons for staying where you are, there are equally doubtful reasons for engaging in the activity of change. Relevant here is Kagan's (1971) wry comment on the characteristic progression of innovation in education:

> An action directed at a goal diverts the mind and aborts the discomfort of apprehension. Our belief in the therapeutic value of work is based on this idea.
>   This principle also helps us to understand the behavior of teachers and administrators who have been made uneasy by the critical attitude of both parents and press toward the school's practices and apparent failures. Educators are anxious because they are not sure what they should do. This anxiety has led them to become preoccupied with change in any form as a way of buffering the uneasiness.
>   Many school systems eagerly await the announcement of any new curriculum, and a great deal of busy work follows. The new curriculum keeps teachers, principals, and supervisors occupied. They

are doing something, and this activity keeps anxiety muted. As might be expected, many teachers and administrators have developed a motive for devising new curricula. For the act of constructing, perfecting, implementing, evaluating, and finally discarding curricula dilutes uncertainty and becomes an attractive goal in its own right.

Some aspects of innovation in educational psychology might plausibly be ascribed to such anxiety-driven behaviour.

Because the educational psychologist is a *social* scientist and practitioner working through other people, the success of changes in practice depends upon his ability to formulate the ideas and principles involved so that they can easily be grasped by the people who need to use them, as well as the development of ways of working that are both credible and acceptable. We are some way from this desirable state and the interim vulnerability is an uncomfortable one.

One of the paradoxes we are faced with is that whilst many people in related professions — education, medicine, administration and so on — may not regard educational psychologists as particularly useful, they often regard their traditional activities as valid and meaningful (Hibbert, 1971). This is probably because accounts of learning and behaviour in terms of 'low ability' or 'learning disability' or 'neurosis' or 'maladjustment' provide powerful and simple explanations which at one level make a great deal of sense and lead to fairly straightforward solutions — even if these do not seem to work out in practice. The difficulty is that potentially more productive ways of working involve ideas that are more complex, and less easy to grasp and communicate than traditional concepts. Hence the need for a deliberate policy of consumer education if we are not to be defeated by a mismatch between expectations and what is being offered.

Both communication needs and the requirements of a school-community approach to children's problems mean that the psychologist has to be able to get to know his schools well and informally — and to stand up to the close scrutiny of familiarity. This has implications not only for staffing ratios in psychological services *but also for the range of work the educational psychologist takes on.* So many problems are psychological, by comparison psychologists are so few. Humanitarian motives, because of their character, are difficult to discount or disregard but their promptings can lead to a form of practice that achieves nothing of real worth. If we want to avoid the fate of the child guidance movement, we must sort out what is distinctive and *useful* about our contribution to the welfare of children: our only justification lies in that direction.

2 THE HISTORICAL DEVELOPMENT OF SCHOOL PSYCHOLOGICAL SERVICES

Tony Dessent

The behaviour of professional groups, no less than the behaviour of individuals, can be usefully viewed in terms of a historical/developmental perspective. In the case of the professional group of educational psychologists, which is increasingly coming to question the nature of its role, such a perspective is necessary in any attempt to understand current practices and philosophy. Radical change within the profession will only be possible in so far as such change can take account of the formal and informal requirements which historically have come to define the role of psychologists working within school psychological services.

Sutton (1975) has attributed the present constitution of psychology in the country to two recent historical trends — the economic boom of the sixties and the particular explosive growth in the late sixties and early seventies of the white-collar 'helping professions'. While the history of psychologists working within the education services can be traced considerably further back than this, Sutton's comments do serve to emphasise the fact that the employment of professional psychologists has been intimately linked to broadly based economic development in society. Cyril Burt's appointment as school psychologist to the London County Council in 1913, the accepted historical landmark of services in this country, and those that followed in the 1920s and 1930s can be seen as a direct consequence of social and economic changes which subsequently came to be reflected in terms of educational provision, thinking and practice.

The process of industrialisation in Western societies during the early nineteenth century produced a complex technology and an elaborate division of labour. It became apparent in England that a socialised, 'educated' work force was required in order to fulfil the needs of industry and of the military machine required by a great power. The Elementary Education Acts of the late nineteenth century which established universal compulsory education reflected both this economic need and the growth, among the privileged classes, of philanthropic attitudes towards the under-privileged. As Burt (1964) himself records, the need for a psychological service in the schools arose with

24

the introduction of the 1870 Education Act. Up till then the voluntary schools had been able to reject the duller and more troublesome children if they wished. The new school boards were not permitted to do so and the school system had to absorb a large number of children who were to experience learning difficulties in the formal educational setting. Interest in this group emerged because they interfered with the 'payment by results' method of determining teachers' salaries (Crowley, 1936). Even when this system was no longer operative the new schools were regularly visited by the school inspectorate and pupils were examined to see how many failed to reach the 'standards' imposed by the Board's Code. Burt (1957) comments that the proportion of failures remained high and teachers began to insist that many of the pupils were inherently incapable of rising to the Board's requirements and that 'not a few were warped beyond reclaim in their mental and moral constitution'. There was an increasing recognition from both the teaching and medical professions that some form of special provision was necessary. Legislation quickly followed. The needs of blind and deaf children had been recognised as early as 1839, and in 1899 the Elementary Education (Defective and Epileptic Children) Act created a new category of handicap. 'Defective' children were defined as 'those children who by reason of mental or physical defect are incapable of receiving proper benefit from the instruction in the ordinary public or elementary school, but are not incapable by reason of such defect of receiving benefit from instruction in special classes or schools'. Under the Act, authorities were empowered to ascertain the number of defective children in their area and to provide for them.

The development of special school facilities for the 'educable mental defectives' raised the problem of how such children could be identified. As Brindle (1975) notes such a problem did not exist prior to the introduction of universal education, since only the grosser forms of mental deficiency, recognisable by unsophisticated observation appeared to have difficulty in adapting to societal demands. The job of selecting and certifying the so-called 'defectives' for transfer to special schools fell, not surprisingly, to the medical profession.

Pritchard (1963) and Kirman (1965) provide examples which suggest that medical officers relied on the presence of physical signs, such as malformation of the head and the presence of 'signs of nerve weakness' in order to distinguish the feeble-minded from the normal population. Their verdicts encountered strong criticism from teachers, parents and education officials. It is interesting that Burt (1964, 1957) gives as one of the reasons for his appointment as the first school psychologist the inadequacies of the medical profession in coping with school placement decisions. He states that 'the certifying doctors . . . tended to pass on every backward youngster', with the result that some after a brief period in the small classes of a special school were returned to normal schools. The cost of special schooling was nearly three times as high as the cost of normal schooling and 'the Education Committee complained of the expense, the parents complained of the stigma and the inspectors and the teachers complained of the faulty diagnosis'. The teaching profession felt that the decisions about placement should be made by someone with 'educational or a psychological experience' rather than 'merely a medical training' (Burt, 1964).

Thus the need to develop 'objective' methods of selection for special schooling arose, and herein lies the historical origins of educational psychology. The pioneering work of men such as Galton, Binet, Pearson and Burt provided the beginnings of a psychometric technology and with it some useful means of tackling the problem. In 1884 Galton had established his anthropometric laboratory where his intention was to examine the mental characteristics of people, as well as their physical characteristics. Galton first advocated the scientific study of the individual pupil, and mental testing, rating scales, biographical schedules, the normal curve and statistical tools like correlation and factor analysis resulted from his work. Galton influenced many scientists of the time including Alfrède Binet who became a member of a Commission, established in Paris in 1904, whose aim was to establish selection methods which would distinguish between the normal population and the 'mentally deficient'. The investigations of Binet and his colleague Theophile Simon led to the development of the Binet-Simon scale for the measurement of intelligence and Binet was able to demonstrate that the typical subjective assessment of mental deficiency was extremely unreliable. It fell to the German educationist Wilhelm Stern to suggest that the ratio of mental age to chronological age could be used to express an *intelligence quotient*, and thus was born the practice of IQ testing which came to define so heavily the role of psychologists within the education services.

At about the same time that Binet was working in France, Cyril Burt submitted a lengthy paper to the British Journal of Psychology which claimed to demonstrate, on the basis of experimental results, the practical value of newly devised 'tests of intelligence' as methods of diagnosing inborn mental differences. With the adoption of the Binet-Simon scale into England, IQ 70 became accepted as the cut-off point between normality and deficiency. As one Senior Medical Officer at the

Board of Education maintained, 'all children with IQs under 70 urgently require special educational facilities similar to those provided in special schools' (Crowley, op. cit.). Thus, the conjunction of the need for special education and the means of mental measurement can be regarded as the historical roots of the profession of educational psychology .

On his appointment to the LCC Burt's duties were numerous but priority was given to the problem of 'how to ascertain educationally subnormal pupils using psychological tests and other scientific procedures' (Burt, 1957). Moreover the link between educational psychologists and ascertainment procedures for special education has been reinforced rather than weakened since Burt by official government policy. The Education Act of 1944 which provides the basis of the contemporary approach to special education served to perpetuate the role of the educational psychologist in ascertainment procedures, with its creation of the concept of educational subnormality and its de-emphasis of the need for medical certification in cases of transfer into special education. More recently, Circular 2/75 (DES,1975) has introduced radical procedural changes in this area which has brought to an end special school placement decision-making by medical personnel: 'It is therefore more appropriate that an experienced educational psychologist or adviser in special education should . . . assume responsibility for conveying to the authority a recommendation about the nature of the special education required and where it should be provided.' Educational psychologists have thus come to fulfil certain quasi-statutory requirements within the Education Services particularly in relation to special educational provision and, as Maliphant (1974) notes, local authorities have often been satisfied to employ psychologists as 'psychometric athletes' in respect of these requirements.

While the development of special educational facilities and the mental testing movement provided the initial impetus for the development of school psychological services, the manner in which services have evolved has been heavily influenced by the particular contribution of early workers such as Burt. Burt was early steeped in Galtonian lore and the study of differential psychology with its emphasis on the hereditary basis of mental and physical characteristics. He had studied under McDougall at Oxford where his special topic was the standardisation of psychological tests. The concept and measurement of 'general intelligence' was to be an abiding interest for Burt. As early as 1909 he wrote: 'The experimental determination of the mental characteristics of individuals is admittedly a problem of wide theoretical interest and of vast

importance. The particular mental character which in importance is
perhaps above all supreme, is that traditionally termed "general intelligence".' During the years that Burt held the LCC post much of his
time was devoted to the adaptation and construction of tests. The results
were published in *Mental and Scholastic Tests* (1921) a classic work
which contained Burt's London revision of the Binet-Simon scale,and
his tests òf educational attainment. However, as Hearnshaw (1964)
comments Burt was never simply a tester; he was always more interested
in the results of testing, practical and theoretical, than in the tests
themselves. His appointment was initially for three years and was half-
time, the other half being left free for psychological research. His
duties and terms of reference (see Keir, 1952) although focused on the
assessment and ascertainment role, were wide and Burt (1964) maintained that the work of an educational psychologist was essentially that
of a scientific investigator and researcher. Burt's own prodigious
research interests both reflected and reinfòrced the dominant conceptual framework of the time. Thus within his work there is an emphasis
on diagnosis, classification, epidemiology and a concern to locate the
'causes' of backwardness and deviant behaviour, an approach which
until recently has strongly influenced psychological research and the
practice of educational psychologists (Tizard, 1976). In his work with
individual cases Burt also developed a scheme for studying and reporting
on children (Keir, op. cit.). Teachers made reports on the individual
pupils they submitted for examination, care committee visitors reported
on the home conditions and when necessary, the medical officer
was asked to make a report on the child's physical condition. Having
reviewed the information in these preliminary reports the psychologist
then interviewed the parents at his office and 'carried out a comprehensive study of the child's intellectual, educational, emotional
and moral characteristics using standardised tests, observations in a play-
room and where appropriate . . . diagnostic teaching'. Thus Burt
produced a method of approach which later was to be adopted in
varying degrees by the services which followed.

   It was, in fact, not until 1931 that the next psychologist was
appointed by a local education authority — the City of Leicester. At
this time also the child guidance movement, with its emphasis on a
multi-disciplinary approach to the guidance of children with problems,
began to get underway. The origins of child guidance are variously
traced to the setting up of a consultancy with a cross-discipline
approach by De Sanctis in Italy in 1899 and to the foundation of the
Chicago Juvenile Psychopathic Institute by Healy in 1908 (DES, 1968).

Burt (1957) maintains that like mental testing the idea of child guidance originated in England and was introduced into America by J.M.Cattell, who was one of the first of Galton's fellow workers. The first demonstration Child Guidance Clinic opened in America in 1920 with aid from the Commonwealth Fund of America with its aim, 'to develop the psychiatric study of difficult, pre-delinquent and delinquent children in schools and juvenile courts and to develop sound methods of treatment based on such a study' (DES, 1968). The Child Guidance Training Centre, also with financial aid from the Commonwealth Fund of America, opened as a clinic in 1929, and in 1932 the first LEA Child Guidance Clinic — consisting of psychologist, psychiatrist and psychiatric social worker — was established in Birmingham. Growth of clinics in Britain was rapid and by 1939 Hearnshaw (op. cit.) records seventeen clinics maintained and five partly maintained by LEAs, as well as a number of others attached to hospitals, universities or of independent status. By about 1944 there were more than seventy child guidance clinics in Great Britain. In terms of organisation the clinic teams were usually headed by a medical director (psychiatrist) who had case responsibility and took the major diagnostic role. The educational psychologist worked mainly with children in schools or aided the psychiatrist's diagnosis by administering psychological tests, with the psychiatric social worker having the responsibility of obtaining background case histories from the child's parents. The Underwood Report (1955) set up to investigate the needs of maladjusted children saw this kind of clinic team as the central feature of a comprehensive child guidance service operating in conjunction with a school psychological service and the school health service. In those areas in which educational psychologists divide their services between the child guidance clinic and the school psychological service, this pattern of working is still operative although there are wide variations in practice. The medical domination of services and the investment of the treatment function with the psychiatrist has acted as a barrier to the development of psychological approaches to therapy and intervention. As Gillham (1975) notes, the independent development of psychological services is largely due to the fact that educational psychologists have felt constricted in a role just as a member of a child guidance team. Certainly, the historical involvement in child guidance has had the effect of severely limiting their role, largely to that of tester.

Moreover, such involvement has served to perpetuate the role of educational psychologists as clinical paramedical experts seeking to contribute to the resolution of problems in isolation from the social environment which gives them meaning. In recent years the efficacy of child guidance clinics has come under close scrutiny and the shortcomings of the approach have been outlined by several writers (see Tizard (1973), Rehin (1972), Whitmore (1972)). However, while the future of child guidance is currently unclear, and the involvement of psychologists is decreasing, its influence on the development of the role of educational psychologists has been considerable and still involves them in a complex set of expectations and informal requirements which highlights certain kinds of activities to the possible neglect of others.

A major milestone in the development of School Psychological Services and the professional practice of educational psychology occurred in 1968 with the publication of the report entitled *Psychologists in Education Services* more generally known as the Summerfield Report. The working party responsible for the preparation of the report had been set up by the Secretary of State for Education and Science, 'to consider the field of work of educational psychologists employed by local education authorities and the qualifications and training necessary; to estimate the number of psychologists required and to make recommendations' (DES, 1968). The impetus to the report came mainly from the developing awareness of the needs of handicapped children following the 1944 Education Act, and a consequent demand for the involvement of psychologists within the Education Services. As Williams (1974) notes, by the middle sixties the demand for educational psychologists had considerably outstripped supply. It is perhaps for this reason that the recommendations made by Summerfield were largely concerned with questions of training, qualifications, numbers required and the organisation of services, rather than as Moore (1969) commented any 'fundamental discussion of the real nature of the work'. At the time the Summerfield Report collected its data in 1965 there were 326 educational psychologists in England and Wales. The profession was predominantly male and although there were variations in terms of qualifications, training and experience, the standard pattern was of an honours degree in psychology, usually with a training for teaching, some years of teaching experience (20 per cent having one year or less) followed by a postgraduate qualification in educational psychology (60 per cent). The usefulness of teaching experience was in fact challenged by the Summerfield Report and has been a hotly disputed issue within the profession since.

One of the more interesting aspects of the report concerned the survey carried out of the proportion of time spent by educational

psychologists in a variety of activities. The two main types were
'psychological assessments' and 'treating children' within child guidance
clinics and elsewhere. The other types were chiefly consequential —
writing reports, administration, travelling, discussing cases, and so on. It
appears that of their total working time about half the psychologists
spent approximately 10 per cent in assessing children at child guidance
clinics and more than half of them spent 20 to 70 per cent of their time
assessing children in schools and elsewhere. The work analysis thus
showed a preponderance of individual clinical, diagnostic and therapeutic work with little indication of involvements in advisory, preventative or in-service training work. Moreover, the scientific research role
of the educational psychologist so strongly advocated and practised by
Burt received little mention. This emphasis was further supported in
considering the topic of the special contribution of educational psychologists. Summerfield accepted the views submitted by the Association of
Educational Psychologists that their unique contribution lies in the
'assessment of the psychological and educational development and
needs of children; in their work as psychologist members of Child
Guidance clinic teams and as contributing to those discussions of
educational policy where a specialist contribution from the academic
and clinical psychological point of view could be useful'. Wright (1974)
writing almost ten years after the Summerfield data was collected,
comments that these are useful guides and that they have not changed
significantly post-Summerfield, and Williams (1974) in the same volume
regards the Report as providing 'a handbook to the practice of educational psychology in England and Wales at present'.

In the decade following Summerfield a traditional model of the
work and role of educational psychologists appears to have emerged.
Such a model rests heavily on the historical roots of educational
psychology and is well exemplified by the perspective adopted by
Chazan, Moore and Williams (1974) in their text book *The Practice of
Educational Psychology*. Phillips (1971) has provided the most succinct
statement of the educational psychologist's role within this model: 'The
case for a profession of educational psychologists rests not on a broad
selection from the great variety of applications of psychology, but on
one central core of skills and responsibilities; the identification,
diagnosis and treatment of individual children with learning and adjustment problems.' Phillips' view is that these 'essential professional skills'
of an educational psychologist are clinical and that he employs these
skills in clinics and takes them into schools. Within this approach there
is a strong emphasis on the importance and value of psychometrics and

on the role of the psychologist in relation to allocation for special
education. Normative testing in general and intelligence testing in
particular are often regarded as invaluable tools enabling the psychologist to predict, diagnose and classify the 'subnormal', the 'maladjusted',
the 'dyslexic', the 'under and over achievers', and so on. The conceptual
framework adopted within this approach is firmly based on a medical
model. Thus concepts such as diagnosis, prognosis and treatment are
applied directly to psychological variables. Maladjustment for instance,
is regarded essentially as a condition and Chazan *et al.* (op. cit.)
comment that 'there are many children whose maladjustment is unde-
tected', and stress 'the need to screen for maladjustment and establish
criteria for deciding whether children are maladjusted or not'. The
approach also involves a concern to discover the causes or determinants
of behaviour, and causes, like problems, are seen as predominantly lying
within individuals. A major consequence of adopting this kind of
conceptual framework is that educational psychologists have come to
regard their role as being to work directly on and with the individual
referred 'case'. This has meant that their energies have been devoted in
the main to individual casework with the 'abnormal' and the 'deviant'.

As Loxley (1976) comments, 'the traditional school psychological
service is principally involved in the definition of deviance with the
emphasis on the detection and treatment of the abnormal'. This conception of the role of educational psychologists would seem to fit
closely with the expectations of the teaching profession and the
educational administration.

Recent history in the development of school psychological services
has been marked by a growing dissatisfaction with the traditional roles.
Over the past four to five years there has been a spate of publications in
and outside the professional journals which attest to these concerns. The
ineffectiveness of child guidance and individual psychotherapy
(Shepherd, Oppenheim & Mitchell, 1971; Rehin, 1972; Tizard, 1973)
and the conceptual and practical failures of intelligence testing (e.g.
Mittler, 1973; Burden, 1973; Gillham, 1974) have now been fairly well
documented. In addition, the need, in Mittler's terms, for assessment
techniques to 'provide information which can be positively harnessed to
the design of a programme of education and habilitation', has been
reinforced by the Education (Handicapped) Act 1970 which brought
responsibility for severely handicapped children under the local education authorities and thereby increased the involvement of school
psychological services with this group of children.

Important conceptual and practical implications have followed from the development of the behaviour modification approach to problem behaviour (see Gillham, 1975) and from the increasing importance attached to sociological and social psychological approaches to 'deviance' (e.g. Hargreaves, 1976). Tizard's 1976 presidential address to the British Psychological Society pinpointed some of the fundamental conceptual changes which have occurred in modern psychology and which in part underlie the criticism of traditional work in educational psychology. He notes that the research approach which characterised the early work of Burt and others into the diagnosis, epidemiology and causes of delinquency and backwardness was largely misguided in that it ignored almost totally the problems of remediation and providing strategies for intervention.

> We could indeed make a case that the reason why clinical, educational and occupational psychology all failed to make a major impact on the problems to which the disciplines ostensibly addressed themselves, was that for half a century or more they were preoccupied largely with questions of taxonomy, diagnosis, structure, interpretation and cause, to the neglect of *learning* in social situations and under specific, and specified, conditions.

The future directions of school psychological services and the role of educational psychologists are currently unclear. Services evolved in response to broadly based social, economic and educational changes, and their subsequent development was influenced by contemporaneous theoretical and technical developments within psychology itself. The radical changes which many people desire within the profession are likely in the end to be dependent upon similar factors. Educational psychologists are clearly not free to step outside of the many formal and informal requirements that define their role within the education services. However, the value of an historical perspective on the development of a professional group lies in the extent to which it reveals how carefully aligned the thinking and practice within a profession is with the requirements of the social/institutional world of which it is a part.

3 PERSONAL VIEW: THREE INTERVIEWS

Tony Dessent

The process of change within a profession or indeed any context is a difficult one to describe. One way is to present the broad process from the viewpoint of individuals who are working their way through it. For this reason, having taken an abstract historical perspective in the previous chapter, the aim of the present one is to capture something of the *feel* of change.

David Loxley, Andrew Sutton and Frank Carter (themselves all contributors to this volume) are three practising educational psychologists who have become increasingly dissatisfied with traditional practice and role conceptions. The interviews presented below formed part of a wider study (Dessent, 1976) and are based upon transcribed material using a structured interview schedule. Attention is focused on their ideas and thinking on a number of critical issues which bear upon the psychologist's role in the education services and his contribution as an applied psychologist. The material thereby illustrates both the diversity of views and the communality of concerns of three psychologists who are closely involved with the business of 'reconstruction' as well as providing some insight into the variety of experiences and influences which, by their own perception, have led the interviewees to their present position.

Interview 1: David Loxley — Principal Psychologist, Sheffield

David Loxley has worked as Principal Psychologist for the Sheffield 'Psychological Service' (as opposed to the *school* psychological service) for the past six years. Prior to that he was head of the service in Huddersfield and before that he worked as an Educational Psychologist for Norwich. While few practising educational psychologists can be said to have exerted a general influence on practice outside their own authorities, Loxley's ideas and the orientation of the Sheffield service are increasingly becoming more widely known (see Loxley 1974, 1976a, 1976b).

Loxley came to Sheffield mainly because he was attracted by the philosophy and views expounded by members of the educational administration concerning the role that psychologists might play in a local authority organisation. He inherited a service which had very little involvement with schools, was clinic based, and concerned with psychotherapeutic intervention with a small and highly select group of children. However, the administration, in 1970, wanted a different kind of service, one in which psychologists moved out of the clinics and went into the schools, especially the ordinary schools. In Loxley's words the psychologists were to 'act as one of the Authority's agencies for observing what went on in schools, monitoring the stress points, looking at the difficulties the schools were meeting and feeding this back into the administration'. The Chief Education Officer also envisaged psychologists as providing in-service education and a research function as well as contributing to departmental working parties and policy formation groups and the evaluation of policies implemented — in short they were to be involved 'at the centre of the educational process in Sheffield'.

Loxley's view is that because the service he inherited had had only limited involvement with the schools this made it possible for the psychologists to represent themselves as people whose business was not simply to deal with individual cases and thereby encourage 'exponential increases in referrals'. However, he points out that to begin with they had to establish a reputation for themselves and therefore did a lot of individual work in response to school demands but then quickly moved to suggest that where large numbers of similar problems occurred within a school this might be symptomatic of broader problems.

He points out that over a period of a year they have halved the rate of referrals from schools and attributes this to the way psychologists have worked in the schools and the way the schools have come to regard them. Psychologists have visited schools on a regular basis and have been involved in preventative work, 'talking about problems and problem situations, problems endemic to the institution, problems of organisation and curriculum development, dealing with the situation before it gets to the referral stage'. The direction they are moving in is that of looking at institutions as areas of social interaction — looking, not at problem children but at children in relation to parents, teachers, peers, the sociology of the neighbourhood and the organisation and curriculum of the school: a much wider context which leads to a much wider involvement in the community. The involvement with schools consists of work following from and generalising from individual cases and work with special groups of teachers, e.g. probationary teachers, counsellors, remedial teachers. He suggests that such involvement is better when operated at the level of their own institution rather than by setting up formal courses. The work in schools has been directed towards encouraging the expectation that the teacher can handle problems which arise in the future.

Loxley maintains that since other services have changed dramatically over the last few years, it would be an exaggeration to claim that the Sheffield service is exceptionally distinct or non-traditional. He suggests rather that at Sheffield they might have a particular emphasis in that they lean away from the traditional child guidance/psychometric testing pattern and are less involved with treatment, less involved with individual assessment and casework. Thus, while they do traditional work for a proportion of the time, they are 'working in the direction of making psychological services available to the Education Department and the community at large on a much broader basis'. His aims are, to help the education services develop along progressive lines via feedback from fieldwork, from routine work, from in-service education with teachers, and by encouraging the involvement of psychologists in research activities and project work.

Loxley appears to have had ample freedom to develop ideas and the psychologist's role at Sheffield and in this respect he regards as an important factor 'how well read and how far sighted your CEO is, and how interested the politicians are in what you want to achieve'. The biggest constraint he sees as an internal one in terms of the reluctance of psychologists to change and he attributes this to traditional training and role expectations. 'People see themselves as entering the job to do person to person work – helping children in difficulties, and they are reluctant to enter into some of the imponderables in the fields of social psychology, of organisations and systems which are not major role expectations.' Thus he sees 'the conservatism of our own professional group as a major constraint'. This conservatism he links to the moves towards professionalisation in educational psychology which he regrets since he sees it as a move towards narrowing down the job. 'The great haste to professionalise educational psychology is an indecent haste based upon a considerable insecurity about the sort of work we are doing – identification as professional is a way of redefining failure as success.' However, he stresses that, in his view, there is more common ground than disagreement amongst the psychologists at Sheffield. Moreover, there is a great deal of cross fertilisation of ideas and he sees it as a healthy phenomenon to have divergence within a service – 'we all need our views tempering by opposite views'.

Loxley disagrees with the assumption that there is a specialised role for a psychologist working within an LEA. 'We have to accept the fact that the educational psychologist is an incomplete kind of person. He has some skills and expertise which he can bring to bear but these are no use in isolation from other kinds of information and knowledge which he will have to gather. There's not a wonderful sort of being with the title"Educational Psychologist"who can do all these things. You're just an individual with a few skills and a certain amount of experience.' Of the latter, Loxley considers important the wide experience of many different institutions and individuals that the psychologist acquires. Of psychology itself Loxley comments, 'I've never ceased to believe that the broader the coverage of psychology itself you could achieve, the more advantageous this would be to your working in any sort of setting as an applied psychologist, but you've got to be humble about your skills and be prepared to be continually looking, searching and learning alongside the other individuals you're working with.'

In considering more traditional approaches to the job, Loxley points out that while it could be argued that a great many more children could benefit from an approach in which individuals are seen, assessed and investigated in some detail, there is no evaluation to prove that it is really all that worthwhile. His belief is that it is both more effective and more economical to use resources preventatively. He takes the view that the individual diagnosis of a problem is not always necessary and often only tells teachers what they already know anyway. Moreover, he suggests that such an approach, which usually ends with curricular recommendations, the provision of worksheets for the teacher and the inevitable reply from the school that all this cannot be done with a class of thirty-seven, 'falls short of the true responsibility and potential of the job if stopped there or if special education and other resources are sought'. Instead educational psychologists should be involved in regular contact with teachers and explore the possibilities of using the resources of the school itself, for example providing courses on how to use materials and tackling the thorny problems of organisation and timetabling to see if it really is necessary for a school to teach thirty-seven as a group the whole while. He also points out that alongside such schools there are others which are organisationally different, attitudinally different and able to cope with their own problems, and that it is the psychologist's responsibility to attempt to emulate such institutions.

Of psychometrics Loxley says 'I don't feel personally that normative psychometrics has any great value because no new information is forthcoming from these very crude instruments. If you really ask the right questions you get all the answers from the observations of the teacher without actually using the tests. Unlike some I don't see the millenium coming with the new British Intelligence Scale.'

However, it would be incorrect to portray Loxley and the Sheffield service as advocating the relinquishment of work at the individual level. He stresses that, while the service is moving in particular directions (e.g. research, in-service education), there is a 'basic bread and butter part of the job [casework] which cannot be ignored' and 'you can't necessarily solve all a child's problems by dealing with his teachers and with organisational factors because there are other factors in his situation which relate to his family and his early experience. You've got to help him to come to an understanding of himself and this means working with him as an individual some of the time.' Working at the individual level is, he says, 'one perspective which I value and recommend'. Later in the interview he put forward his view of the educational psychologist as someone involved in broad educational issues (e.g. streaming, ROSLA, integration of the handicapped, nursery education): a view which stresses the importance of a broad theoretical perspective, research skills, the capacity to collect, synthesise and analyse information, to design experiments and carry out statistical work, and a view which sees psychologists as 'being in the business of evaluation in education'. But again he points out, 'I don't want to neglect individual kids in trouble, someone's got to be their advocate and very often the psychologist is the appropriate person to do that — so I want child advocacy too.' He suggests that these are not discrete functions — 'they interpenetrate each other and inform each other. Acting as a child advocate you get an idea of what's going on in the system and the organisation which then enables you to evaluate that.'

In considering particular professional duties of an educational psychologist, Loxley's view is that there is insufficient time for a psychologist to be a remedial teacher although he may have to give advice or demonstration on this aspect. As for therapy, he says this is difficult to define and that any interaction can be seen as therapeutic. 'To do it properly you may need a great deal of personal insight and psychologists often don't possess this.' He points to the findings of Truax and Carkhuff (1972) as being important for psychologists and suggests that, 'the role does embrace the need to be understanding and empathic of the situation, not only of the person who is the individual client, but all those with whom he is involved'. As for behaviour modification, he stresses that he is not an expert in this area, but he does have reservations about it, and that it often does not work in practice because reinforcement schedules are not adhered to and because teachers find it impossible to ignore deviant behaviour, and difficult and time consuming to look for desired behaviour in a large class. He suggests that it might be more profitable to change teachers' habitual reactions to pupils, for example by spending some time talking informally to children at registration or in the playground, about something that matters to the child, so as to establish a different kind of relationship between teacher and pupil. He says this is nothing more than good teaching but that we need to draw attention to the fact that such behaviour can overcome a lot of classroom problems by fulfilling the child's attention-seeking needs.

Loxley regards the writing of psychological reports as a contentious area and that, in the end, it is a matter for the individual psychologist to decide. Much depends upon the sort of report it is: thus he sees it as reasonable to write down curriculum recommendations as this is different from a report about a person's personal problems and life which is confidential. 'Isn't it better if you regard yourself as a helper and befriend people, that you should sit and talk to them and listen rather than write reports and official letters?' If reports are used he favours the kind of report which might help bring a situation to life, a narrative type of report which attempts to present 'a slice of that person's life as it interacts with the circumstances in which he finds himself, rather than a report which labels a person and which appears to give a definitive account of a person's personality and potential stamped on him indelibly'.

Loxley considers that his present position is 'a developing thing' — to do with his own past experiences as a psychologist, people he has met and books he has read. He regards his past experience (some of which was of the clinical, intensive casework, projective technique kind) as being influential in establishing the need for a client-centred perspective even within a systems approach, and his previous work in a large immigrant area as emphasising the need to look at what is happening within a broad social-cultural context.

Much of the interview discussion centred around the distinctions between different kinds of psychologists who might work with children, the concepts of a generic psychologist and the idea of Community Psychology. Loxley sees no reason why you cannot have a generic kind of psychologist and he notes he is still impressed by the original arguments of the Seebohm Report for a generic social worker. He is of the view that many of the skills involved in dealing with people at different age levels and stages of development are similar: for example, the problems of handicapped children and the concern to develop the skills of these children via the setting up of Toy Libraries, 'is an exercise which cannot be too far removed from a similar kind of

exercise at the other end of the age scale where skills are deteriorating
and they need compensatory activities and psychological input to help
them keep alert, active and thinking'. Although he prefers a holistic
view he says there is a place for specialists and that there would be
room in his organisation for someone interested in something as
specialised as the development of physically handicapped children up to
six months as well as a place for someone with a broader view. He is
particularly concerned not to have educational psychology with its
broad range of concerns labelled as child psychology. 'You can't allow
this to be called child psychology because you're concerned with a
much broader range; you're dealing with people in further education,
higher education, adult education and hopefully as you extend into
the community there will be educational opportunities, retraining
opportunities and pre-retirement opportunities for ageing people.'
This is his definition of educational psychology which he recognises
might be questioned by others. He bases it on his view that many of
the skills are similar and on the notion of community psychology. He
believes the Education Department is a good base from which to
develop community psychology, especially in a setting where
community education is a big issue and means education for life. He
contrasts this view with that of those who talk about child psychology
and push for the amalgamation of psychologists who work with
children in different settings. He notes that perhaps both developments are possible but is concerned about the extent to which child
psychology models itself on paediatrics and is 'steeped in the medical
model'. However, he is concerned that child psychologists should not
be excluded from working in organisations such as the Sheffield
service. 'I would like specialist child psychologists in this sort of
organisation and I would also like clinical psychologists – there
are areas of a local authority service which could use different kinds of
psychologists and they should be in regular interaction within the same
organisational setting.'

In view of Loxley's community psychology emphasis the client
group to whom services are aimed is necessarily broad – 'Your
clientele is not just the group on your waiting list, it's all the kids out
there, the college students and the community at large.' He is also very
aware of the problems involved in deciding who the client is in any
particular situation, and suggests that the act of referral needs to be
treated by us as a 'reflexive process' so that it becomes possible to treat
the child as the client and the situation and the organisation as the
'case'.

Loxley has particularly well formed views on the nature of training requirements for educational psychologists. He would value psychologists who had a thorough grounding in psychology itself, very much more social psychology and a whole range of experiences, guided and controlled in a range of applied settings. He sees this as preferable or at least as a viable alternative to the 'disappearance into the wilderness of teaching for several years – this bizarre situation which educational psychologists face of having to qualify and practise in a different profession – this is unheard of in any other profession'. He considers this an affront to the teaching profession, 'that we foist ourselves on it with no intention of permanence'. Moreover, he says he receives many unsolicited testimonials from schools concerning the usefulness of psychologists in classroom situations who have had no teaching experience at all. On the whole he thinks that postgraduate training (perhaps end-on to a psychology degree) should last for at least two years rather than one but he is also prepared to accept that you could obtain the equivalent of this in short bursts over a more prolonged period and relates this to Dubin's (1974) concept of the 'half life' in psychology and the deterioration of effectiveness. In terms of the content of training courses he hopes especially that the potentiality of social psychology and the psychology of organisations is going to be capitalised on much more in the future. He also considers that the personal qualities of psychologists (the ability to relate to and work with children *and* adults) are very important and that in so far as it is possible applied psychologists should be selected for these qualities. Loxley comments that in his experience of colleagues' dealings with others he cannot overestimate the importance of insight and understanding of oneself and while he does not advocate self analysis he does suggest that we should try and perceive what is going on between ourselves and the people we talk to.

In terms of changes within educational psychology in the future Loxley considers that there are two possible alternatives. First, the development, he hopes for, of a community psychology orientation, i.e. a multidisciplinary team of psychologists under one roof; and secondly the change he fears, but thinks unlikely, that the 'professionalisation process turns us into some kind of technocrat or technician who is associated with a particular area of education and limited to that particular sphere'. 'I believe that we've got to face the issue of what the psychologist's role is – and the various options within that role – then we should be setting the job on a much firmer footing than we have done in the past, in the sense of communicating what the potential of the job is.'

Interview 2: Andrew Sutton – Psychologist, Birmingham

Andrew Sutton does not fit comfortably into the 'local authority
educational psychologist' mould and although he was trained and has
worked as an educational psychologist he is not happy to be labelled as
such. Following his professional training course at Birmingham in 1965
he worked as an educational psychologist in Newport (Mon.) and in
Birmingham. In 1970 he took up the first joint teaching/local authority
psychologist's post based at Birmingham University and funded by
Birmingham Public Health Department. This gave him responsibility for
a psychological service which worked with the Children's Department
and pre-school children, together with a lectureship. Following reorganisation, his current post with the Education Department includes three
aspects: an educational research role, secondment to work for the Area
Health Authority and lecturing part-time at Birmingham University.
Sutton has also been responsible for bringing together applied psychologists from various fields for a series of formal and informal meetings
under the banner of 'The Movement of Practising Psychologists (MOPP)'
and a series of papers have been produced expressing some of their
dissatisfactions with applied psychology as traditionally practised
(e.g. Sutton, 1975a, 1975b).

In reflecting on his varied work experiences as a psychologist Sutton
looks back favourably on his early work in Newport. 'I fell very lucky
there, it was an exceedingly good education authority and the
psychologist had an enviable range of responsibilities, far wider than
many psychologists have nowadays. I was responsible for the organisation of special education, remedial education, the Child and Family
Guidance Clinic and for the School Psychological Service. It was very
good. I felt that I had some power, and could make decisions and could
do the job to the full, which was exceedingly fulfilling.' He contrasts
this with the way in which most educational psychologists work. 'I can't
see any point in being involved in special education unless you help run
it and say which children go where, what the schools should do and
what the pattern of provision should be in a town.' He feels that Burt's
model was largely correct, 'You saw individual cases to identify a
problem; you informed the authority what was needed according to the
state of knowledge at the time, and then you laid it on. This was my
ideal of educational psychology.' He also adds, 'I'm not altogether sure
that there is a psychology of education available; what most educational
psychologists peddle isn't psychology of education, I doubt whether it's

even psychology, and I certainly don't want to be associated with the
current image of the educational psychologist. If someone asked me
what kind of psychologist I am I'd say a child psychologist or a developmental psychologist . . . but I don't fit into the academic divisions of
the BPS.'

Sutton feels that he now has one of the most advantageous local
authority jobs possible. The Education Department pays his salary and
accepts that he has a research job. Within this context he has carried
out a survey of nine- to ten-year-old ESN(M) children in the city and
has written a report which (a) defines this population – who they are,
how they got there – and (b) describes them in terms of the Soviet
criteria of mental handicap. He believes that the time is coming when
ESN schools may well be closed, 'for lack of interest', but he would
like to see them closed for 'the right reasons'. He is also preparing a
report on educational failure in Asian children and putting forward a
suggestion that these children might be taught in their native language.
Within his work in the Parent and Child Centre (Area Health) he sees
some individual pre-school children and takes an interest in 'weirdness
of personal mental development', but mainly he acts as a consultant to
social workers. Within this context he believes he has learnt a lot: 'more
than anything, I've learnt that you evaluate pre-school children, even
more than you do other children, by getting someone to do something
for them and then seeing what happens'.

Sutton regards the 'traditional' educational psychologist as 'a
marbles-counter, full stop. He's associated with the little blue box:
that's what the teachers expect and want and that's what they get.' He
believes that the stereotype is very strong 'that we can somehow reveal
the innate potential of a child and this is our field, there is no other
field. It's a mysterious thing, but we can do it, and we are called on to
do it to justify the decision-making that is going on.' He criticises traditional services on the grounds that 'they don't provide a service –
they're generating undoable work, and that's no "service". On the
whole it's a service for teachers, a complaints service. There's no criterion established for anything, we rubber-stamp admissions for special
schools and the decision-making is conducted either side of us. We stand
in the middle and affect reality very little.' He quotes some research on
the great variability of children sent to ESN schools (Brindle, 1974)
and remarks: 'That's not a service, it's a matter of public concern.' He
also believes that most of the things psychologists traditionally do
should be done by other people.

Psychologists in the past have made the mistake of trying to make themselves essential to organisations, and that's bad. What you should aim to do is make yourself *unnecessary* to an activity — if we have anything to offer we should be teaching other people to do it. Why do you need a psychologist to put kids in a special school? If there were psychological techniques involved, 'experimentation', then it would be a different matter. Once something stops being an experiment and becomes a technique it's transferable. The psychologist is needed for the funny things, developing things anew. He shouldn't invent a thing and say it's psychology and only psychologists can do it. It has a ludicrous ultimate effect — it dates, and you become a laughing stock. We should be looking for the new things and telling people that the thing we told them five years ago is now out of date.

He believes that what psychologists must not do is 'set themselves up as experts on something and then see everyone in town. You've got to say "Here is how you improve your behaviour: when you've improved we're no longer the experts, you've sapped us dry, we'll come back when we can add to it." '

Unlike David Loxley, Sutton regards himself as in part 'a psychometrist'. 'I believe in technique, it depends what you use it for; I'm after potential, but prediction is the negation of potential. The Holy Grail I'm seeking is to be able to demonstrate relatively convincingly in an English context that apart from those with CNS impairment, the dullest people have infinite potential. You need rigorous psychometry for that, but above that you need the techniques of intervention.' Thus for Sutton psychometrics are essential as a means of monitoring change. 'I look forward to the new BIS, to me it's a liberating thing because, from what I understand of it, I'll be able to measure quite small degrees of change in specific areas.'

The main influences which Sutton recognises on his own thinking stem from his involvement with Soviet psychology. He considers himself lucky that his first degree was in Russian Literature. 'The major influence was reading the original works of Vygotskii; they made me feel very humble. He's a more important figure than Piaget. My whole psychology is now based on them.' He believes that Soviet psychology offers both a viable theoretical and practical alternative to Western approaches. 'It's based on a theory of human development which states categorically that human intelligence and human personality are the product of adult- child interaction. The system was laid down in the

1930s and it had to fit the dictates of the state. It had to meet certain
economic goals and it had to work. It had to raise the intellectual level
of an underdeveloped country.' He regards it as an approach implying
infinite malleability so long as there is an intact CNS and sensory input,
and within the approach there are techniques, he believes, which
enable psychologists to discriminate between those with impaired and
those with intact central nervous systems. 'It's a teaching approach. A
formal manifestation I use is called the "teaching experiment". The
Russians developed it in the early sixties: it's a step as big as Binet's and
we haven't heard about it in the West — a whole new psychological
technology has sprung up for measuring potential — you set a goal and
you teach a new mental tool which can then generalise to other situations.' The aim of this approach, to measure 'potential', seems similar to
that of traditional intelligence testing, but is conducted against a vastly
different theoretical background.

> In our system potential is measured by the level of present develop-
> ment. The Russians say that in a growing person there are two levels
> of development: the level of present development, how much he
> knows, what he can do unaided, that's what you measure with
> traditional IQ tests; and secondly there's the level of potential
> development, what he can learn to do with the best help of an adult
> — when you measure this you realise you're measuring a new dimen-
> sion, the dimension we are really interested in, the teaching dimen-
> sion.

Sutton suggests that when the technique is applied in ESN(M)
schools he finds two groups of children. 'First, those children who,
however you teach them, cannot attain the goal and even if by some
chance they parrot it you can't get them to generalise what's been
taught to a similar task.' This group he considers to have 'a damaged
CNS' and to be therefore mentally handicapped (from his own survey
he believes this to be at the most 40 per cent of the ESN(M) population).

> You can also see some really 'stupid', ignorant kids and you can
> teach it to them as quickly as you can teach your wife because
> they're intact — and you can teach them something new easily. They
> don't know anything, they're ignorant, deprived, unhealthy and ill-
> taught and they have all these things reinforced as they grow older.
> You can give them a WISC and you get 58 or 63 and you have to
> work yourself to death, but teach them something new and it's quite

different. Assess by intervention, a cliché that we all know. The
difference comes in the practice.

He believes that we give this group of children an 'honorary brain
damage' label and that the Russians regard our ESN categories as a joke.
'They think that what we do is an absolute shambles because they say
we impede the education of both groups.' Sutton feels that we need
separate educational goals for these two groups of children and different
places of learning: 'I want mentally handicapped children to leave
school reading at the ten or eleven year level, but I want children who
are culturally deprived at seven with WISCs of 63 to leave school with
their 'O' levels. I want neither on the scrapheap.'

Sutton sees the unique contribution of psychology as an applied
discipline in that it offers the potential, already realisable if we tried it,
of making the activities of our social institutions more scientific. He
believes that as a society we invest vast sums in influencing human behaviour but that we do it on an *ad hoc* basis rather than empirically
validating what we do, and he regards this as preventing us from developing the theory to generate effective activities. 'The process I see is
from practice, which we evaluate, to theory that generates new practice
and so on. At the moment practice is determined by all sorts of things
but rarely by that.' He regards the study of development as being about
change and the effects of intervention. 'I want to intervene and change.
Soviet psychology has a marvellous parable which says the child is like
a garden and we are the gardeners. If you just allow the child to grow up
willy-nilly, as he would in nature, you get what you get if you let nature
grow up anyway — just plain ordinary weeds. You've got to cultivate
the growth and shape your garden.'

He also maintains that we already have some useful theory 'to make
some suggestions about how events might be modified straight away,
and the means to evaluate whether there's been a real change, a chance
change or a change due to other factors'. Thus he feels that we have an
experimental methodology and we have a few tools, 'but our basic tool
is experiment, and the object of experiment is mental and intermental
processes'. Sutton suggests that the Soviet model 'that all *intra*personal
phenomena exist initially as *inter*personal phenomena' offers viable and
useful practical approaches and is an improvement on 'he's got an attack
of the Ids, or he's got a complex, or he's ESN or low IQ'. He finds that
the other useful model we've got is the simple experimental model. As
an example he gives the mother who brings her four-and-a-half year old
and asks if he will be able to cope with normal school because of the

problems she has had with him. 'You can go and look at the kid and give him tests but there's no possible way of knowing whether he can cope with infant school even if you know the school. You say, "Well, try it out." That may sound obvious but you must point out that often the only way of predicting the future is to get into the future and look back at what has happened.'

While Sutton sees children mainly at home or at school, he believes it is essential also to have purpose-built facilities in which children can be seen. 'You need to be able to take a kid somewhere. For the sort of kid who almost certainly carries his abnormality around inside him you need a neutral situation and you need equipment. I want to define a kid's abnormality as closely as I can. You can learn a lot about some kids in a silent room with everything to hand.' He stresses that the real value of such a facility lies in its potential for experimentation and developing new techniques. 'I'm thinking about psychologists working to find out new things and trying them out, not just dealing with problems as they arise.'

When asked what kinds of changes he looked forward to in the future, Sutton's reply was 'More cuts. What's happening in local government is that people want to know what they are paying for. Out of all local government staff we're the most vulnerable. What are people getting for their money? We've inflated the training, inflated the salaries, got vast numbers of people coming in, a contracting school population, a contracting teaching population and contracted local government expenditure. We're in trouble. People are going to ask what we do, what we've done and what we've got.' He looks forward to psychologists being accountable for their activities and his main fear is, 'That I'm going to be judged on the bad practice of others, providing "services for teachers", filling in the SE3s. What else need a psychologist do, a lot of young people think it's not bad for £5,000 a year, you don't have to think.'

Interview 3: Frank Carter – Senior Educational Psychologist, Nottinghamshire

At the time the interview was carried out Frank Carter worked as an Educational Psychologist for Cheshire based in Ellesmere Port. He is a practising Roman Catholic who originally came into psychology with strong philanthropic attitudes and intentions. He found academic psychology full of jargon, and largely irrelevant to contemporary needs and issues, and after graduating left university 'disillusioned' wondering how to use what he had learnt 'to help mankind'. Consequently he applied to the British Volunteer Programme and was taken on to teach in the East African bush. Since then he has completed his formal professional training in the UK and taught for a further four years in the Remedial Department of a large West Riding comprehensive, subsequently becoming an LEA educational psychologist. Now he finds himself grappling with the problems involved in trying to decide what kind of work educational psychologists should be doing.

Carter is highly critical of traditional school psychological services which he defines as:

Accepting referrals of individual children mostly from schools and from head-teachers rather than class teachers in particular. Dividing those referrals into two groups — behaviour and learning problems, and tackling those referrals with what the psychologist knows best — his psychometric kit, hoping that by applying psychometrics he might quickly get information that it would take longer to get by other means; judging what is best for that child on the basis of his findings with a psychometric test and on the basis sometimes of class teachers' observations or parental interview and usually making a recommendation along the lines that the child is 'underachieving' and therefore needs something to bring his achievement up in line with his potential.

He thinks it is basically a model which 'searches for referrals, stacks them one on top of the other, and knocks them off one after the other working from the top downwards and occasionally juggling with the order. But mainly trying to influence the aptitude of the individual child for coping rather than trying to influence parental strategies or classroom and school systems.'

This kind of approach he regards as 'a fundamental nonsense because you're just piling up referrals. Most schools only refer when they think it's the end of the road, when they've tried everything they can think of. The problem is pretty well entrenched; the psychologist just adds it to his list and it can then be any amount of time before he does anything about it and that's assuming that what he does will be effective anyway.' He regards the idea of a waiting list approach as an unfortunate product of a hospital consultancy model and prefers the system which he operates of dropping what he is doing to give immediate attention to a problem in the belief that immediate attention can defuse a situation. He contrasts this with the traditional set up which exists in his old authority where a client's name, date of birth and age is taken by a secretary and then placed on a waiting list.

Carter also believes that one has to search hard to find the psychology in what educational psychologists traditionally do. 'It's very much the kind of psychology with a small "p" — Reader's Digest type psychology where the layman says, "he applied psychology". It's kiddology and sadly unscientific. I don't see much in the way of behavioural science operating.'

Carter formulated three areas in which he believes psychologists could make a more profitable contribution. First, an approach 'developing useful objective assessment techniques with a view to remedying skill deficiencies by providing appropriate remedial teaching'. Carter believes that normative testing has very limited value but that criterion referenced approaches such as those of the Hester Adrian Research Centre (Language Developmental Charts) and the Gunzburg Progress Assessment Charts are useful because the criteria are quite explicit and give an idea where the child has reached and give the teacher and parent a clear idea about what the next step is. 'Basically what I'm after is this method. I think it's much more useful because you need to look at the child as a developing being rather than having a typology approach which I identify with standardised IQ tests.'

A second contribution he believes in: 'Opening up a debate with the educational administration as to what the problems are in an area, using surveys and screening to obtain incidence rates and then putting the information to the Administration and evaluating what the authority sets up — this is a fair contribution for a psychologist.' Thirdly he proposes the approach which he has been most closely concerned with: 'Getting involved intimately in certain schools, doing a fusing job [by which he means fusing the view of all the people involved with the child as to the nature of the problem], attempting to modify attitudes and behaviour.' Within this approach he believes the direction of attack has got to be centred much more on the family and parental participation, 'teachers and parents pulling together, each defining together what they want for a particular child. I still see myself being concerned with individual children but I think the implications are that we should be class based and family based.' In working with parents Carter appears to adopt a behavioural approach. 'I personally feel quite committed to an operant model because it does clearly specify events and the contingencies around the event; these are simple concepts for parents to work with.' Carter points out that all of these three areas of potential effectiveness 'have in common the business of being known and getting to know a specific area [in the community] — this is the crucial bit'.

Carter regards his previous working experience as an educational psychologist as the major influence on his present thinking: 'There's something satisfying about performing the traditional role — it's easy and it's quite good fun putting kids through a battery of tests, forming hypotheses about performance and so on. I did that for a while and chipped away at a waiting list. Then I came to a point where I realised that I was much more acceptable in some schools than others. I knew more about some schools and felt more effective in them. It's a matter of being aware of the "colour" of a school — the ethos — aims — relationships.' He saw this as being of some significance for the way he was going to work. He found that although his initial involvement in such schools was to carry out psychometric assessments, it turned into an involvement where schools just wanted to talk with him about problems. He was able to clarify issues, 'to talk on the same plane', and able to recommend different teaching approaches, to be a *part of decisions* rather than *imposing recommendations.* In connection with this, he thinks it important that psychologists carry out classroom experimental work, 'pushing up suggestions for teachers to try out'. He thinks that this approach of intense involvement in schools works largely because an aura of confidence is engendered — 'Caring is a word I use to describe what happens.'

Carter's comments on aspects of an educational psychologist's work, such as report writing and in-service education are particularly interesting. Report writing 'where relevant' is, he believes, a very personal thing. 'It helps me to structure my thoughts about individual children. They should be written in a good English style — my criterion is, can I show this to the child's parents? If the answer is no then I write another one.' (In the past he has had some conflict with colleagues over his desire to show reports to parents.) He believes that in-service education in the form of courses for teachers run by psychologists is usually a flop. He is personally more committed to in-service work being 'in-classroom work', which is situation specific. Carter is also a strong advocate of psychologists being research orientated and points to a small-scale research project which he instigated in one school on identification and intervention with children with problems in the area of social skills and language. He maintains that this had important spin-offs — first, it revealed that head-teachers can identify children-in-need 'intuitively' and without the need for extensive testing, the point being that the teacher may well have the relevant information, but has not structured and systematised it so that it is accessible and hence usable. Secondly such a project had the effect of getting teachers to look at children differently — as developing individuals — rather than just as 'good' or 'bad'. And thirdly it aided in the organisation of paraprofessional help in the school.

Carter is sceptical about the usefulness of much of the academic training that psychologists receive and regards psychology as 'just a primitive science getting underway'. He considers the study of child development and experience of working with children as important aspects of training. The former because he finds it useful to see people as developing beings: 'It's helpful to bring about changes if you can get people to see children in this way; developing implies that progress can be made and changes can be made'; and the latter because he thinks sensitivity towards children is vital although such experience, he feels, need not necessarily be gained by teaching experience.

In considering the special contribution of psychology as a discipline to an LEA, Carter points to the fact of its being the only behavioural science operating within education but adds 'psychology has value in that it poses the appropriate questions'. He thinks there are some hopeful areas especially the concern of psychologists now with *learning* as opposed to other processes or invariables like personality. 'Psychology is the only profession concerned with learning, and education is concerned with learning. If psychology can get into the business of identifying how particular children learn in particular situations then we've got a hell of a contribution.' He looks favourably on the work of Bruner, in attempting to put forward a theory of instruction and of Piaget, 'who calls out for a scientific pedagogy and whose concern is for the developing individual and adapting schooling and learning to the individual child'. However, he does not think psychologists are applied workers in the same way as medical workers.

I don't feel we are — it may be the root of the error that psychologists have got into by behaving as though there really is an academic psychology which accurately defines behaviour at all stages, as physiology does to medicine, so that we have a cookbook which we can turn to — we don't have a counterpart to physiology, behaviour is not compartmentalisable and explicitly definable. What knowledge we have is not generalisable across all fields. My strength as a psychologist is in Ellesmere Port and in other areas I know quite well. Perhaps being a psychologist comes down to being 'a nice guy' and someone who is prepared to look closely at behaviour.

4 MEDICAL AND PSYCHOLOGICAL CONCEPTS OF PROBLEM BEHAVIOUR

Michael Roe

> ... when I meet a small child I always take it for granted that, within
> his limited sphere of activity and given his own premises, he is logical
> ... my problem is to understand what his expressions mean, and
> hence grasp his existential situation ... From this point of view,
> people are always seen as logical (rational) given their own premises,
> and hence behaviour can, in principle, always be understood.
> (Smedslund, 1977)

We talk about maladjusted children but not about maladjusted adults.
Adults are neurotic, psychotic, silly or criminal but not maladjusted.
Yet when we look around at other people, or at ourselves, we see far
more foolishness and self-defeating behaviour than we ever see among
children. Children, given their immaturity and lack of experience, are
more rational and sensible than most adults: what they lack in understanding they make up for in straightforwardness. It is the charm of
Lewis Carroll, himself a logician, that he captured precisely the discon-
certing logicality of children. Children are consistent: they think as they
act and act as they think.

Why then do we separate from other children a group we call
'maladjusted', 'emotionally disturbed' or 'anti-social' and classify others
as suffering from 'behaviour disorder'? Is what they are doing somehow
different from ordinary childish behaviour? When other children behave
so rationally, are they in some way behaving irrationally? Is there something essentially different about them, something abnormal? In place of
so much order, is there disorder?

I will argue in this chapter that children who are called 'maladjusted'
(or by any of the other names) are acting as reasonably as other
children, that their behaviour is normal childish behaviour, and that
their emotions and behaviour are as orderly as those of other children;
and that when we try to understand them in terms of dislocated
emotions or disordered behaviour we make a verbal smudge which
obscures what can be plainly understood.

Many psychologists have asked themselves what all the children they see have in common. One answer (and it is not entirely trivial) is that in every case some adult is worried about the child and is not sure what to do. We might go one step further and say that:

— some of them are struggling against real life situations which no child could be expected to cope with;
— there are some who have never learnt necessary skills;
— most of them have dug themselves into holes they do not know how to climb out of.

Maladjustment is a medical problem and is dealt with by psychiatrists: it is a 'psychiatric disorder' (Committee on Child Health Services, 1976). On the other hand there are difficulties variously called 'cognitive' or 'educational' which are properly dealt with by educational psychologists. How does this curious bifurcation arise? Why are emotions and some sorts of behaviour medical, and learning and other sorts of behaviour non-medical? The answer lies in history.

Seeking to help the patients who brought their problems to him, Freud, a neurologist by training, saw an analogy between their complaints and the symptoms of physical disease. Beneath these symptoms, which his patients could not account for, there must be some underlying and hidden cause, some malfunction of the psychic apparatus, which the physician could uncover by patient investigation. Just as a bilious feeling is explained by some disorder in the liver, so a guilty feeling may be explained by some disorder around the repression barrier. Freud was both the anatomist and the physiologist of the psyche. He was not the first to draw the analogy, but he used it more thoroughly and brilliantly than anyone else. It is mainly because of his prestige that we find it hard to rid our minds of the notion, however vague, that psychological troubles are in some way of the same kind as physical diseases, and thus chiefly a medical concern.

This is the medical model in its strong form. In this form, the medical model of maladjustment is now, if not a dead horse, at least scarcely worth the flogging. We accept that maladjustment is not a disease (Rutter, 1975): in place of disease entities we have 'factors' and 'clusters'; in place of biological progressions we have 'family dynamics' and 'situational determinants'. The study of the anatomy of the psyche is out of fashion.

But are we any better off? Freud was a rigorous and thorough-going worker. His system was well anchored in the analogy between bodily organs, which we know well, and psychic organs that cannot be observed. And if some of what he dug up was fool's gold, at least it

glittered. Cut off from his analogy we flutter around vaguely and grasp
at something which, if not the same, looks something like it. If we
cannot have diseases, we can have disorders; and if the disorder is not
precisely located somewhere within the child, at least he somehow
wears it round him like an aura. We can still use the vocabulary —
patient, onset, aetiology, prognosis, diagnosis, syndrome, therapy — and
this helps to steady us. Our new thinking retains (to use a Piagetian
term) adherences from the old. Maladjustment is an abnormality; we
can isolate it, study it and, if possible, cure it. This is the weak medical
model.

We can regard the weak medical model as a compromise — a civilised
arrangement that has enabled us to live in uneasy peace with our
psychiatric colleagues. But it has two serious disadvantages. One is
that it separates problems of feeling and behaviour on the one hand
from problems of learning on the other. The second is the assumption
that what we are dealing with is abnormality, and hence something
foreign to normal human experience and the field of general psychology.

The first, the separation between learning problems and problems of
emotion and behaviour, is especially pernicious. There are of course a
few children whose backwardness in reading and writing can be traced
to a rare cognitive deficit. There is also a definite and stubborn correlation between the ability to learn to read and that strange intellectual
quality we call intelligence. But these things aside, it is hard to see
where learning problems end and emotional or behaviour problems
begin. We know, for instance, that there is a relationship between
reading attainment and such remote social variables as social class,
position in the family and so on (see, for instance, Rutter *et al.*, 1970).
These must operate mainly through their effect on the child's self-
esteem, his level of aspiration, his motivation and his style of living — all
things we deal with when we are dealing with maladjusted children.
Many stubborn reading problems, too, fit neatly into the notion of
'learned helplessness' which Seligman (1975) relates to adult depression
— an authentic emotional condition. Most experienced psychologists
and remedial teachers, in fact, know that the first step in remediation is
to re-establish the child's faith in his ability to tackle a learning
situation. But the separation of learning problems from those labelled
'psychiatric' has led many psychologists to transform their art into a
kind of technology, in the belief that if only one looks hard enough,
and uses plenty of tests, one is bound to turn up a cognitive deficit of
some kind to explain this reading problem. Remedial centres are made
to look like laboratories, tiny deficits in sequencing or short-term
memory are made to explain huge reading deficits, and whole remedial

programmes are made to balance precariously on them. Then, when backwardness is found in association with undeniable problems of feeling or behaviour, we are led to ask such meaningless questions as: 'Is he backward because he is maladjusted or maladjusted because he is backward?'

Sometimes the distinction is broken down, but only at the expense of assimilating backwardness to maladjustment. After eliminating the dull (who are considered beyond help) and the lower working class (who are considered beyond hope) the rest are subjected to 'educational therapy'. This is sometimes merely an eccentric way of saying remedial teaching. But whereas some remedial centres look like laboratories, others look like playrooms; little or no teaching goes on in them. The idea is that the emotional problem is primary and must be got rid of before any teaching is done. As this process is apt to be a long one, the child gets further and further backward and hope is further and further deferred. This, no doubt, is what the Court Report (op. cit.) means when it talks about 'educational medicine'.

The second misconception goes even deeper and is more persistent. This is the assumption that what we are called on to deal with is abnormal behaviour, abnormal emotion and the like. The implication is that something pathological has intruded into normal child development and distorted it. This may be a particular network of family dynamics, a failure of bonding or something of that kind; but whatever it may be, what it has produced is a 'maladjusted' child, an abnormal child. He may not have his 'psychiatric disorder' in quite the same way as he might have measles, but he is a child 'with' psychiatric disorder (Rutter *et al.*, op. cit.) Take him out of the situation which has produced the disorder, and he still 'has' it (though a process of 'spontaneous recovery' may take place). His behaviour seems bizarre, unreasonable, unusual, ineffectual or self-defeating; it must be separated from normal child behaviour and studied as a phenomenon in its own right. Therefore, we have a phenomenon and a programme to investigate it. Like Pasteur on the track of the rabies micro-organism, we first trace the pathogenic factor and then produce a specific cure. As it is difficult to see what the bully has in common with the timid boy he drives under the table, we first map out the phenomenon in all its varieties (we produce a taxonomy — see for instance, Stott *et al.*, 1975; Rutter, 1965) and from then proceed to prescribing specific treatments.

But all children have problems, and all parents have problems with children. In adopting the notion of maladjustment, we set apart one set of childish troubles from all other childish troubles; one field of study is separated from the field of general psychology. The student turns from books on child development to books on maladjustment. Much of this chapter is concerned with arguing that this is an artificial bifurcation. There is another point. Whatever we may think about theories of maladjustment, people bring children to us, complain loudly and expect us as psychologists and teachers to do something about it. If, as I argue, these problems are problems of normal child development, these adults are setting problems that normal child development must encompass. This is an important challenge to psychological theory. What has it to say, for instance, about autism? Much psychological theory seems to have been developed in academic isolation uncontaminated by the vulgar complexities of human beings. But I doubt if we should know so much as we do about theories of metallurgy if wings had not started falling off aircraft and mechanics had not started shaking their greasy fists.

In recent years, many psychologists have dismissed from their minds the medical model in both its strong and weak forms; with it they have dismissed the whole concept of maladjustment. On the face of it, this is a bold step. We have books on maladjustment, conferences on maladjustment, teachers of maladjusted children and maladjusted schools for them to teach in; maladjustment is an official DES category; there are several journals devoted to maladjustment bristling with case studies. Furthermore, we have theories of maladjustment, to say nothing of taxonomies. Is this all wasted effort, tantamount to the anthropological study of the Hobbit? I think not. Children who worry and children who worry us there certainly are; what is proposed here is merely a different way of working for them and thinking about them. Chemistry owes much to the alchemists.

The *psychological* view can be summed up in a few propositions:

1. What Has Been Called Maladjusted Behaviour is Normal Behaviour

Fight, flight, stealing, lying, feelings of inadequacy, truancy, fears, sleep disturbances, jealousy — all these are so commonplace in childhood (and, indeed, in adulthood) that they must be regarded as a normal, though unpleasant, part of everyday living. We could not apply the term 'abnormal' to them without asserting that all children (and most adults) are abnormal some of the time. This observation has been made many times, for instance by Valentine (1956) and Pringle (1974). The latter goes on to explain that we should regard these normal bits of behaviour as maladjusted when, for example, they persist for a long time, are particularly intense, or occur at the wrong age. This is, so to speak, an attempt to save the notion of maladjustment against the odds. It fails for several reasons.

It is reasonable to fight — and go on fighting — if one is cornered by enemies. It is equally reasonable, if one can, to run away and hide. It is reasonable (if illegal) to steal if one is cold and hungry. Many adults when they feel hard-done-by or neglected go on a shopping spree to cheer themselves up: in children we call this 'symbolic stealing' or 'stealing for love'. Harassed teachers sometimes play truant. In our society an irrational distaste for eating human flesh is considered normal, and Bowlby (1975), with characteristic acuity, challenges us to think again about so-called *irrational* fears in general. For it is neither the abnormality nor the intensity of the behaviour that attracts attention and makes people complain: it is the context in which the behaviour takes place. Suppose we see a child putting up a vicious fight. If he were hemmed in by a gang of bullies, we should commend his courage. If he were in a group of inoffensive children, the same behaviour would seem odd. If a child refused to go to a thoroughly unpleasant, cold, disagreeable school, we might upbraid him, but we would understand him. If we knew that the school was a healthy, well-conducted, friendly place, we might take him to see a psychologist. When we describe behaviour as 'maladjusted' we are making a judgement about situations.

2. What We See is not Disorder but Order

It is generally true of the children who are drawn to our attention that they are remarkably predictable. A backward child reliably and monotonously fails to learn. You can rely on another child to put his fists up on every occasion (and his blows have the smoothness of skilled action). You know where to look for the withdrawn infant: he is in the Wendy house. In terms of predictive validity, educationally subnormal children are a gift to the makers of tests. It is the children we never see who are full of surprises. The same observations apply to emotions. What is an 'emotional disorder'? Emotions are not disordered, they are just emotions. One suspects that people use the word 'disorder' merely because they do not want to use the word 'disease': it is a way of saying that we have abandoned the strong medical model and embraced the weak. To use it in this context is to do violence to the English language.

3. The Child is Doing His Best in the World as He Sees It

If you ask a child why he is doing something, he usually gives a reasonable explanation. The school refuser gives a convincing account of the horrors of his school. When he tries to bring home to an experienced shoplifter the error of his ways, the psychologist finds his exhortations sounding very lame in face of the well-thought-out justifications of his client. When it comes to reasonable explanations, children beat adults every time.

This is the psychologist's classic dilemma. The behaviour he is called in to deal with seems irrational; but he finds himself up against a well-articulated structure of beliefs and feelings. One way of getting out of it is to reject the child's explanations as 'rationalisations': the beliefs are constructed by the child to explain his feelings or justify his emotions. This is the kind of theory often invoked in psychology to explain such puzzling phenomena as racial prejudice. In the case of the maladjusted child we are inclined to say that the anger, or the fear, came first and, like the maker of myths, the child builds up the picture of a hostile world to justify his own feelings; the rationalisation is a kind of unconscious lie.

But there is an alternative, and that is to turn the proposition upside down: the belief in a hostile world causes the hostile feelings. When he justifies his conduct, the child is telling the truth; and what he gives you is a picture of the real world *as he sees it.* In this world his feelings and his actions are, even to our eyes, perfectly reasonable. This is the assumption of normality. There is nothing radically new in this assumption. It is used in the study of prejudice, for instance, by Tajfel (1973). It is particularly the view of those who accept the insights (if not necessarily the system) of George Kelly. In a much-neglected paper, Ravenette (1972) applies the same reasoning to troubled children and makes use also of concepts derived from Piaget. The advantages of this method of thought, however, are less often argued. These will be considered in a later section.

4. Many Children Dig Themselves into Holes – and are Kept There

Unsuccessful forms of behaviour tend to maintain themselves because they affect the actions and feelings of other people. (The same may be true of successful forms of behaviour as well, but with this we are not concerned.)

A great deal of attention has been paid recently to the interaction between parents and children, which is now seen not to be all one way even in the very early days of childhood (see, for example, Bell, 1968). There are, as we can tell from common observation, similar effects in the interaction between child and child. Children do not suffer patiently for ever; the aggressive child finds himself in the end surrounded in real earnest by enemies, and he has no alternative but to fight his way out. If his initial assumption is that other children are menaces, he will find his belief confirmed every day. A miserable, withdrawn child is a wet blanket: why should other children go out of their way to meet him? Many children pilfer because the world seems to withhold its goodies from them: they will be punished by being further deprived. Most teenage delinquents seem to see the adult world as mean and punitive; and when we catch them we go out of our way to prove them right. Even teachers are human and perhaps without realising it tend to give more attention to the child who learns and responds.

Besides, once one has built up a picture of the world, a theory, it is painful to abandon it. Eminent scientists in their youth propound fine new theories, and spend their declining years defending them stubbornly, long after they have ceased to be of any use. Children are no different. It is a common observation that if children who feel rejected are put into the company of adults who manifestly accept them, there is a period during which they seem to be doing everything possible to court rejection. Their theory of adults is not so easily abandoned. When you try to persuade a backward child that he is not a dunce you expect him to be pleased and to accept this welcome news; but you usually find that his work deteriorates for a while afterwards. With teenagers, in particular, pride is often involved and prevents an easy change of mind. If all you have had to pride yourself on for years is your place as head of a playground protection racket, it is painful to give this up for the uncertain compensations the psychologist holds up before you.

Thus children dig themselves into holes. Some holes are more comfortable than others. Sometimes it is the child who tries to get out of the hole and finds himself getting in deeper. Sometimes he finds the hole very cosy, and it is only the adults around him who call for pick and shovel. In either case, the psychologist is the patient digger.

One advantage of the psychological model is that it is hard to apply; it forces one to think things out; it may even seem paradoxical. A child is brought to us because he is constantly fighting his classmates. He tells us that they pick on him and will not let him alone. We look into it and find that his classmates are, in fact, a friendly, peaceable lot who get on well with each other. Another child disrupts lessons. He says that the lessons are boring, that his teacher keeps picking on him and ignores him even when he tries to do a good piece of work. We know her, in fact, to be a successful teacher liked by her class, who has always gone out of her way to encourage him. A third child is miserable and withdrawn. He hates school because the other children are stuck up and will not talk to him. But we know many very friendly children who like the school and do well there. So we have a series of contradictions: how can we resolve them?

The easy way out is to say that one child has a behaviour disorder, another an emotional disorder and so on, and that we can ignore what they say as rationalisations. We can then set about treating the child for this disorder in the hope that as a by-product his 'perceptions' will become more 'veridical'. The difficult way out, but the more fruitful, is to accept the child's account as truthful, as a veridical account of the child's world, even if it is not the truth as we and others see it.

In real life we accept that different people see things differently. Put an artist, a civil engineer and a geologist at the foot of the same mountain and then compare their accounts of what they see; where the artist sees a beautiful landscape the engineer may see an ugly obstacle. Neither is lying. Two people return from a fortnight's holiday in the same resort: one finds it gay, exciting and stimulating; the other finds it tawdry, noisy, garish and depressing. In Browning's *The Ring and the Book,* three sets of people relate the same facts in the same order, and the three accounts conflict radically. If one child says that his classmates are bullies, another says they are good companions: each has his point of view.

If we accept the child's account of his world — and we can explore it in many ways — we begin to see that a child's feelings and actions make perfect sense. It may be that the techniques he has at his disposal are limited (fighting may be all he knows), but he uses them as best he can in the circumstances. If we think that his behaviour or his emotional reaction is excessive, we misjudge the situation; if we think it is persistent, we ignore the effect he has on others; if we think it is crude or primitive, we forget he is a child.

The second advantage of the psychological model is that it puts the problem into the context of general psychology. Our intellectual roots are in this field. We should not turn from our study of social psychology, the psychology of learning, developmental psychology and cognitive psychology to some alien subject which is called variously 'abnormal child psychology' or 'the psychology of maladjustment'. We should be free to apply what we know about children as psychologists and about people as human beings.

There is space here for only a few hints on how general psychology can be applied to common problems. One of these is the problem of teenage delinquency. A host of conditions have been shown to be associated with delinquency; but these — divorce and separation of parents, inconsistent and harsh punishment, low social class, educational backwardness — are remote social variables which, in themselves, explain nothing. We might do better to explore, on the lines of Piaget (1932) or Kohlberg (1963) a youngster's level of moral development. Bearing this in mind, we might consider then why inconsistent discipline, for example, should be a factor in 'producing' delinquency. If we take Piaget's basic argument in its simplest form, we might say that a child comes to understand the world by observing invariances in the flux of experience: intelligence grows by assimilating – and accommodating to – lawful variations in a generally lawful world. If the world is inconsistent, if an act disapproved of one day is either ignored or even praised on the next, then the building up of judgements, especially moral judgements, will be extremely difficult. The child will cling to very simple, immature judgements and strategies, because these are the only ones that are frequently confirmed; hence the immaturity that we often find in delinquents.

In the same context we might ask why harsh discipline is often found in association with delinquency. One obvious answer is that delinquent acts attract harsh discipline anyway: this no doubt is part of the story. On the other hand, we might invoke the work of Latané and others on bystander apathy (Latané and Darley, 1968) and put it together with work on modelling (Bandura *et al.*, 1963). One interpretation is that when someone is in a situation he is not sure how to handle he watches what other people do and does the same. If we were suddenly transported to a ball at Buckingham Palace we should do precisely that. Growing up is a process of coming to terms with a succession of situations that are puzzling and hard to handle. So the child watches what other people do and builds up his repertoire of behaviour by doing as they do. When he is not certain as to how to interpret a situation he listens to and observes others and interprets it in the same way. It is not surprising then, that children who come from homes where discipline is harsh are apt to learn that harshness is the appropriate way of handling threatening situations, and they may have no other in their repertoire. If he interprets the world as a harsh, punitive place then he will act accordingly.

The same reasoning applies to the known relationship between backwardness in school and low social class. It is often said that poor children come from unstimulating homes and that this is why they are backward. The opposite is usually the case: these homes are frequently more stimulating than the average suburban semi. But the stimulation is often random and unpredictable – lacking the rhythm and lawfulness that form the ground of intellectual growth. Under stress, mother's temper is unpredictable; father may be depressed by unemployment one day and aroused by sudden affluence the next. Noise, that antidote of misery, surrounds him — the television in the living room, big sister's record player in the room next door. When home is too miserable, he is sent out to play in the hurly-burly of the streets. Learning is the elaboration of invariances: there are too few invariances in his life for him to elaborate.

These are trivial examples. But we see no 'pathogenic agents'; we only see children growing up, and behaving, and learning, in different environments just as we would expect them to from our knowledge of general psychology. Then why are topics such as 'backwardness' and 'maladjustment' set aside from general psychology? And why is general psychology so neglected when people come to write on these topics? Why is it so rarely pointed out that the 'causes' of 'bad adjustment' are precisely the same as the causes of good?

One of the most important contributions of the behaviour therapists was their insistence on getting the problem as clear as possible in their own minds and in those of their clients (see, for instance, Wolpe, 1973). They taught us to reject such vague terms as 'aggressive', 'withdrawn', 'school phobic', 'dyslexic', 'electively mute', and to get down to finding out exactly what the client did (or could not do) on what occasions and under what circumstances. They and their successors, the behaviour modifiers, defined behaviour in this rigorous way because it helped them judge what techniques to apply, the ideal being a tailor-made programme,

But that is not the only advantage. Freud called dreams the royal road to the unconscious. We might say that behaviour was the royal road to the child's world. If we accept that a child's behaviour is his normal and reasonable way of coping with the world in which he lives, then we have only to observe his behaviour and ask ourselves the question: 'In what world would this behaviour be reasonable childish behaviour?' If he has failed to learn to read over the years and every day has been a failure, then any reasonable person would either decide he was stupid and withdraw, or seek self-esteem elsewhere; we should not expect children to be heroes. Dr Johnson defined an ambassador as a man sent to lie abroad for the good of his country. Many children lie for their own good — in the world of adults they are likewise foreigners and deviousness is obligatory. Like Kipling's rowdy soldier, the so-called 'deviant' child is 'remarkably like you'.

We also talk to children, and we would be well advised to listen to what they say. Children do, of course, lie, but it is my experience that they rarely lie to people they trust; what they say is their truth, which may not be quite our truth, but it is as true to them as our truth is to us. It is not until much later that children learn to lie to themselves or even achieve 'rationalisations'. In this process, techniques such as repertory grids and questionnaires have their place. It would be foolish to abandon intelligence tests; the main objection to them is that they take a long time and are boring to administer except when they reveal some unexpected discrepancy. But these instruments are useful only when collated with information from other sources and made to fit into a pattern. At their worst, in the hands of an incompetent psychologist, they are useful only in cloaking a lack of ordinary human understanding.

Do we sometimes forget, when we meet a backward teenager, to ask him why he is backward? Do we forget to explain to an anxious child why we have been asked to see him? Do we always ask a disruptive pupil for his own account of the facts? If we are thinking of some form of treatment, do we explain what we intend to do and why? Do we tell him what all these tests are supposed to be about?

In almost all problems of education, behaviour or emotion, we have two things to do: restructure the child's world and teach him new skills. The two almost always go together. Most backward children not only lack the skills of reading and writing, they also see themselves as hopeless dunces and reading as a highly esoteric mystery. Most withdrawn children not only see the world as full of threatening people, they also lack the skills needed for gossiping and playing rough games. Many aggressive children are weak in diplomacy. Treatment is not a matter of removing something, it is an educational enterprise in every way.

Many forms of treatment used by psychologists are based explicitly on one or other form of learning theory. Others are the more or less remote descendants of psychoanalysis. Still others are based on the cognitive model advocated in this chapter. All are useful. For consistency's sake, they can all be made to fit in to one general view of psychology. 'Eclectic' need no longer be a synonym for 'sloppy'. There is now a multitude of techniques for teaching new skills, for instance, remedial teaching, social skill training and assertion training (see, for instance, Krumboltz *et al.*, 1969). Relaxation methods (Jacobson, 1938) also, presumably come under this heading. What is not often pointed out is that these methods are essentially the traditional methods of the concerned teacher, refined, controlled and brought up to date. It is not always realised either, that, as Ravenette (op. cit.) points out, the child is an element in his own world, and by changing his behaviour, and his view of himself, the psychologist also helps the child restructure his world.

Techniques such as non-directive therapy (Rogers, 1951) are, paradoxically enough, a much more direct attack on the child's cognitions. Made to explain your view of the world and the people in it to an adult (who at best expands on what you say) forces you to think hard about what you believe. It is a variant of the old maxim that the best way to learn about anything is to teach it to someone else.

One can, on the other hand, set out doggedly but humanely to disconfirm the child's view of the world. If, as suggested above, children dig themselves into holes and come to be treated in such a way that their idiosyncratic view of the world is continually confirmed, then one way of altering the situation is to act in an unexpected way. No child can hold out for ever though his reluctance to change may provoke what used to be called 'resistances'. Successful remedial teaching contradicts his view of himself as a dunce. If he is used to attracting attention by misbehaving and being ignored when he is quiet, we need to reverse the situation. Many successful schools for 'maladjusted' children operate by sticking to the child through thick and thin, thus contradicting the child's view of himself as the kind of person others reject.

Anyone who deliberately interferes with the style of life of another person is taking a risk. We have all at times questioned our right to do so. In the case of children the ethical problem is particularly acute for it is not usually the child but some adult who has asked for help. In the small hours we remember Huxley's Brave New World — a world of people conditioned to live the kind of life to which one can apply one's favourite term of abuse — conforming, conventional, bourgeois, consumerist, ant-like — whatever it may happen to be. The very word 'adjustment', if that is the opposite of 'maladjustment', evokes pictures of ourselves training a child to accept the values and behaviour of a world that is quite obviously mad. Deprived of his obsessional visions, Blake settles for turning out pop lyrics and pictures for sale in the Kings Road.

We should not worry so much. I once knew a lady whose job was to look after under-age prostitutes. She was not particularly concerned to turn out virtuous women — that would be a bonus; she felt that she had scored a success when one of her charges became a respectable kept woman. She had a point. We do not aim to produce conforming children, happy children or contented children. We try to dig children out of the holes they have dug for themselves and let them go. We try to expand their field of choice. It is not for us to choose whether a particular child becomes a successful guerrilla or a successful capitalist tycoon. Treatment is a scaffolding: once it is removed, the building should stand on its own.

It is here that the existentialists have a point (Frankl, 1973). We are in the habit of regarding children as the product of genetic endowment and environment – and of nothing else. Perhaps psychology can be made to work only if this simple assumption can be made. But assumption it is; and by carrying it into the real world we may adopt attitudes that harm our work with children. By robbing a child, in thought, of his ability to choose we reduce him to a mechanism, a victim, a product that comes (badly or well made-up) off the assembly line. If we adopt this attitude when dealing with a child he may come to adopt it himself. What I am asking for is a humane look back at the schoolmasterly attitudes that have been so despised in recent years. Treatment should aim to hand back to the child, as soon as possible, responsibility for his own actions with all that implies in terms of approval and blame. Schools which employ contract methods are I think working towards this. Workers such as Eichhorn and Homer Lane clearly had this principle at the back of their minds.

No treatment will be successful unless, in the end, the child finds satisfaction from a new way of acting. The backward reader needs to discover that reading can be pleasant and useful. The delinquent needs to discover that virtue, if not always its own reward, is at least a worthwhile possession. The 'fisty' child needs to find the satisfactions of sharing. To put it in the jargon, treatment cannot succeed unless, at the end, extrinsic reinforcement gives way to intrinsic. Forced brain-washing is no more permanent than other forms of cleansing (Lifton, 1961). The hero of *The Clockwork Orange* would soon have lost his conditioned response to Ludwig van. This point, first made by Allport (1937) forty years ago, has not been reiterated often enough.

Most important of all, treatment should lead to what has been called 'reprogramming the environment' (Patterson *et al.*, 1967). It is the argument of this chapter that so-called 'maladjusted' behaviour is sustained by the effect it has on other people. If a child begins to behave differently, so will other people. The child's new view of himself and the world will be constantly confirmed.

But there is another side to this argument. It is the strength of our profession that, being so busy, we have to work through other people: individual treatment is a luxury. So methods of helping the child are worked out in discussion with other responsible adults who have daily contact with the child. This is a double advantage. In the first place, it returns to parents and teachers skills in the upbringing of children that are properly theirs and which psychologists have no right to expropriate. In the second place, it increases their confidence and sense of competence. It is a fair inference from the work of Shepherd and his colleagues in Buckinghamshire (Shepherd *et al.*, 1971) that parents who felt competent in handling the problems of their children did as well on their own as those who felt less competent and took them to child guidance clinics. It is also a fair inference from the work following the Plowden Report (see DES, 1975) that working-class children did poorly in school, not because their parents were stupid, ignorant or lazy, but because they had less confidence in their ability to teach their children. In the past, psychologists and psychiatrists have done as much as writers in Sunday newspapers to undermine the confidence of parents and teachers. It is time they started to repair the damage.

5 DEVIANCE: THE INTERACTIONIST APPROACH

David Hargreaves

My concern is with labelling theory, which is more accurately described as the interactionist approach to deviance. This perspective is rooted in social psychology and sociology, and more particularly in those schools of thought known as symbolic interactionism and phenomenology. One of the best (though by no means earliest) expositions of this interactionist perspective is that of Howard Becker (1966), who writes:

> Deviance is *not* a quality of the act the person commits, but rather a consequence of the application by others of rules and sanctions to an 'offender'. The deviant is one to whom that label has been successfully applied; deviant behaviour is behaviour that people so label . . . Whether an act is deviant depends on how other people react to it . . . Deviance is not the quality that lies in the behaviour itself, but in the interaction between the person who commits an act and those who respond to it.

We can see that this perspective is interactionist and relativist. It is interactionist in that deviance arises not so much when a person commits a particular kind of act, but when that kind of act is perceived, defined and labelled by some person or audience (which may, of course, include that person himself) as deviant in nature. Deviance is a social definition and a social product. The perspective is relativist in that acts cannot be described as deviant in any absolute sense. Deviance is relative to who commits the act, in what kind of situation, before which audience. Public nudity (e.g. 'streaking') is defined by most people as deviant; semi-public nudity (e.g. a nudist colony) is defined by many fewer people as deviant; and private nudity (e.g. in one's own bedroom) is defined by very few people as deviant in our own age. Nudity can be deviant and non-deviant; for us to know whether nudity is deviant we need to specify who is naked, when, where and in whose eyes.

Stated in this way, the interactionist approach may seem very reasonable and uncontroversial to you. Yet the implications jeopardise the foundations of many psychological approaches to deviance and challenge the working assumptions of those adhering to these psychological perspectives. A simple example would be the view, common among psychologists, that there exist in our schools certain pupils who are 'mentally subnormal' or 'maladjusted' and that the task of the psychologist is to locate them and then initiate appropriate provision for them. Such a working assumption conflicts with the interactionist approach, which asserts that such pupils are, strictly speaking, not 'mentally subnormal' or 'maladjusted' until someone (here, the psychologist) actually defines or labels them in such terms. In other words, labelling theory denies that the psychologist is merely locating persons who were in fact 'mentally retarded' or 'maladjusted' *prior to* his discovery and labelling of them. Instead, labelling theory asserts that in a sense they *become* mentally retarded only when they are located and labelled. The 'in a sense' is an important rider, for labelling theory is obviously not asserting that the labelling of a pupil as 'mentally subnormal' changes, say, neuronal functioning in the brain. The pupil becomes 'mentally retarded' in that certain aspects of him, notably his mental functioning, are transformed and given new meaning by the new label. His family, for instance, may have labelled him as 'a bit slow for his age', a label which does not have the same meaning to most people as 'mentally subnormal' which is an official category with a rather specific meaning and social significance. It is in this sense that he becomes mentally retarded by the action of the labelling. We can see at once that these differences in assumption, viz:

> Psychologist's assumption: a certain proportion of pupils in the schools is 'mentally subnormal' and my job is to locate those pupils and help them;
> Interactionist's assumption: there are certain kinds of pupils (who behave in certain ways and are defined by teachers and pupils in certain terms) who come to be located by psychologists and labelled by them in particular ways with particular consequences;

— lead to major differences in the way the phenomenon is to be examined, investigated and analysed. Each approach regards different aspects of the phenomenon as problematic, with the consequence that very different kinds of analysis and research are undertaken.

For the educational psychologist, one of the most significant implications of the interactionist approach is the threat that is offered to the medical approach to deviance. The links between educational and medical psychology are very close; indeed educational psychologists

receive what is often described as 'clinical training' and usually work
closely with psychiatrists. It is true that there are fundamental
differences between undergraduate courses in academic psychology
and equivalent courses in medicine and that educational psychologists
become experts in areas such as psychometrics and cognitive remediation rather than psychoanalysis or chemotherapy. Nevertheless there
seems to be within the profession a strong orientation to clinical,
psychiatric and psychotherapeutic work. One has the impression that
many educational psychologists are uneasily suspended, in a state
of status ambiguity, between the worlds of academic psychology and
clinical psychiatry.

These role ambiguities and conflicts are not to be alleviated by the
interactionist approach to deviance, some of whose adherents have
made a fundamental attack on the notion of mental illness. A central
figure in this argument has been R.D. Laing, himself a psychiatrist, but
since he has been ostracised by the majority of psychiatrists there are
considerable risks for any educational psychologist who espouses an
overt Laingian position. Within labelling theory itself it is probably
Thomas S. Szasz, especially in his book, *The Myth of Mental Illness*
(1961), who has made the most elaborate and extensive critique of the
concept of mental illness. With such a provocative title it is hardly
surprising that Szasz has provoked as much misunderstanding and
hostility as critical scrutiny of his thesis. His argument is not to deny
that people we define or label as 'mentally ill' are specifiably different
from those we define as 'normal' or that such persons have greater
problems than most in coping with their everyday lives. If that were his
argument, it would be self-evidently absurd. Those we call 'mentally ill'
do indeed break social rules of our culture; their acts are seen by
others as incongruous, inappropriate and even incomprehensible. In
terms of labelling theory, which defines deviance as perceived rule-
breaking, such persons do indulge in deviant conduct. As I understand
Szasz, the argument is not that such persons are not deviant, but that
it is inappropriate for the audience (whether they be psychiatrists,
psychologists or laymen) to conceptualise that deviant conduct as
'mental illness'. It is the *disease* analogy implicit in the concept of
'mental illness' to which he takes exception. Thus he writes: 'I hold that
mental illness is a metaphorical disease; that, in other words, bodily
illness stands in the same relation to mental illness as a defective television receiver stands to an objectionable television programme.'

We cannot, according to Szasz, make the transposition from bodily
to mental illness with the same analogy without distorting, misrepre-

senting and misconceptualising the phenomenon of deviance. In this transposition from the body to the mind, from physical functioning to social functioning, the medical analogy carries with it the whole conceptual apparatus of symptom, syndrome, diagnosis, aetiology, pathology, therapy and cure which are for the most part inappropriate for understanding or explaining social deviance and therefore inadequate as a basis for programmes designed to eliminate that deviance.

In his later writing Szasz attempts to expose the imperialistic tentacles of psychiatry which transforms an enormous variety of forms of social deviance into forms of mental illness. Criminals, delinquents and homosexuals are now held to be 'sick' and in need of 'treatment' rather than punishment. Armed with its apparently humanistic ideology, psychiatry converts all our prisons into potential mental hospitals. And if survey figures on homosexuality and self-report studies of delinquency are to be trusted, it is clear that at a stroke psychiatry now defines most of the population as more or less 'sick'. This is the scope of psychiatry's 'humanism'.

In rejecting the medical model of mental illness — and I do not have space to document the details of the attack — Szasz offers the alternative model of the *game*, which he believes is a more appropriate analogy for the understanding of the phenomenon that we call mental illness. In *The Myth of Mental Illness* he sketches an alternative interpretation of hysteria as a non-verbal communication game with its own rules and language. In exchanging models, the phenomenon of deviance is conceptualised in ways which highlight the inadmissibility of notions inherent in the medical analogy. Let me give just one illustration:

> Let us assume that the problem of hysteria resembles the problem of a person speaking a foreign language rather than that of a person having a bodily disease. We think of diseases as having 'causes', 'treatments' and 'cures'. However, if a person speaks a language other than our own, we do not look for the 'cause' of his particular linguistic behaviour: it would be foolish — and fruitless — to search for the 'aetiology' of speaking French. To understand such behaviour we must think in terms of *learning* and *meaning* . . . It follows that if hysteria is regarded as a special form of communicative behaviour it is meaningless to enquire into its 'causes'. As with languages, we shall only be able to ask how hysteria was *learned* and what it *means*.

I do not know how many educational psychologists still hold to the medical analogy in defining and treating the conduct of pupils referred to them. Presumably a relatively small proportion of the school population as a whole is ever categorised as 'mentally ill' and diagnosed as psychotic, schizophrenic, etc. But it is interesting to speculate on the number of pupils dealt with by educational psychologists that are perceived as or officially categorised in terms such as 'maladjusted', 'disturbed', etc. and are responded to in terms of the medical analogy. 'Maladjustment' may not be a 'mental illness' in any strict sense, but it can certainly be conceived within the medical model and carry the relevant conceptual apparatus of 'diagnosis', 'symptom', 'aetiology' and 'cure'. Certainly some labels (e.g. school phobic) fall much more naturally within the scope of the medical model than others (e.g. school refuser). It may be, however, that many educational psychologists, including those who prefer a psychoanalytical orientation, may employ the medical vocabulary in a fairly superficial way, as part of an historical heritage and as part of a conscious attempt to legitimate themselves in relation to their psychiatrist colleagues. One must accept the possibility, in the absence of relevant research, that the medical model may not permeate psychologists' basic notions of pupil deviance. In that case they are certainly closer to Szasz's own position, as well as to many others who are part of, or who closely ally themselves with, labelling theory. One thinks here of Laing's work on schizophrenia and the nature of family relationships, and the work of Edwin Lemert, a central figure in labelling theory, on the nature of the interpersonal relations of the person who is defined as paranoid. This classic paper (1962) is an excellent illustration of the labelling theorist's emphasis on the way in which deviance is generated within a social context, and the way in which the conduct of the person who ultimately becomes defined both formally and informally as deviant represents an adaptation or adjustment to that situation and its very real social pressures. Lemert shows that a person who ultimately gets defined as 'paranoid' really is subjected to a subtle and complex process of social exclusion. But if some educational psychologists conceive of 'maladjusted' or 'disturbed' pupils in similar terms, the common ground between them and labelling theorists is still no more than superficial. The existence of common ground must not be denied, but it must not blind us to the major differences.

Terms such as 'maladjustment' are defective in that they fail to specify to what or whom the person is maladjusted: the situation in which the deviance arises and the audience which accomplishes the ascription of deviance are ignored. The labelling theorist would be suspicious of the diffuse nature of concepts such as 'maladjustment' because they imply a generalised condition that is abstracted from its social context. 'Maladjusted-to-his-teachers-and-in-the-eyes-of-his-teachers', is an imputation that contrasts interestingly with 'maladjusted-to-his-peers-but-only-in-the-eyes-of-his-teacher-and-not-in-the-eyes-of-parents-peers-or-offender'. The educational psychologist, of course, makes such distinctions in practice. The nature and source of the 'maladjustment' may be crucial to a psychologist with a psychoanalytical orientation; and he may take great pains to construct an appropriate case history to determine the pathology.

To the educational psychologist with a preference for behaviour modification techniques — to take just one example of a different kind of educational psychologist — the sources of the 'maladjustment' may be of little interest. His objective is to correct the faulty learning, to extinguish existing patterns and replace them with patterns which are more adaptive. Here we have come some way from the medical model. Our Skinnerian educational psychologist certainly avoids the labelling theorists's objections to the medical model, but he also ignores several other elements which are of central significance to the interactionist.

In defining a pupil as maladjusted, the educational psychologist tends to locate the 'problem' *within the individual* who has come to be defined as deviant. The source of the problem may in part lie outside him — in his family and his early socialisation at home, at school and in the community — but in a sense he can be said to 'own' the 'problem'. It is thus largely on him that reformative procedures are centred; it is he who is having the problems, and they will disappear if he changes. It is true of course that often the teacher too is changed in that he may be taught behaviour modification skills to effect the change in the pupil. There is here an implicit criticism of the teacher in that it could be held that the child's problems spring directly from the teacher's failure to handle him appropriately in the first place. In a more radical view the 'problem' could be located in the teacher rather than in the pupil. That is, it is not so much that the pupil 'has' problems but that he *makes* problems and he makes them for the teacher. Doubtless some educational psychologists sometimes come close to such a view and are willing, like some head-teachers, to speak of 'problem teachers' as well as 'problem pupils'. But it is generally presupposed that teachers cannot be 'maladjusted'; there is no formal provision for sending them to the educational psychologist by a process of official referral. Teachers are, quite simply, much more powerful than pupils and ascriptions of 'maladjustment' to them dare not be made overtly unless formal certification of mental illness is a possibility. Only children (and perhaps adults in the least powerful sections of society) can be subjected to these sub-psychiatric labels. Should an educational psychologist overtly define a teacher as maladjusted, he would risk provoking a stigmatising label on himself from an irate and affronted teaching profession. Educational psychologists are truly intended to be child psychologists only. So if the educational psychologist does locate some of the problems in the teacher, he must approach the problem with considerable social skill and tact.

But the price of such diplomacy is high. The teacher himself will persist in believing one basic assumption of the medical model, namely that deviance is to be located within individuals. He does not have to give up his belief that the 'problem' is really the child's problem, and that his own problems in dealing with the child are merely a product of the child's problems. His new success in coping with the deviant pupil can be explained in terms of his own acquisition of new skills and a new therapeutic role within his own classroom. In short, I detect in the Skinnerian position a potential movement away from the medical model towards a more interactionist position, but the shift in position is superficial in the educational psychologist and leaves the teacher's common sense adherence to the medical model intact.

A fully interactionist perspective would require a much greater change in the educational psychologist's conception of deviance. Labelling theorists insist that deviance does not arise until some audience labels it as such. The acts themselves occur to be sure, but their interpretation as *deviant* acts is a social construction. This is evident in the writing of all major theorists. Thus Erikson (1962) writes:

> Deviance is not a property *inherent* in certain forms of behaviour: it is a property *conferred upon* these forms by audiences which directly witness them. The critical variable in the study of deviance, then, is the social audience rather than the individual actor, since it is the audience which eventually determines whether or not any episode of behaviour or class of episodes is labelled deviant.

In similar terms, Simmons (1969) writes:

> Deviants do not exist in nature, but are man-made categories. This means that deviance is not an inherent attribute of any behaviour but is a social process of labelling. Society is the creative force behind the deviant. This does not mean that there is no such thing as deviance or that the deviant is just an innocent bystander. It means

that society is an active partner in producing the phenomenon
called deviance and that we must look at the work of both partners
if we want to understand.

The implication, if the labeller is the most crucial variable, is that we
can learn at least as much about deviance in school if we look at the
definers of deviance, the teachers, as if we look at those who are
defined as deviant, the pupils. This is so because it is by looking at the
teachers that we shall discover:

(1) what kind of teachers
(2) in what kind of schools
(3) define what kinds of pupils as deviant
(4) because they commit what kinds of act
(5) which break what kinds of rule
(6) on what kinds of occasion.

This kind of information could be acquired only very indirectly and inadequately from pupils who are defined as deviant. The challenge of
labelling theory to the educational psychologist is that he look to the
labelling process rather than at the *labelled product.* It is not enough
to consider one partner to the interaction (the pupil) and ignore the
other partner (the teacher) completely except as a source of information about the deviant or as a means of therapeutic help. Further, not
only does the educational psychologist focus his attentions so heavily
on the product rather than the process, but he also accepts the legitimacy of the labelled product. He does not normally see the defining
and referral process as itself problematic and in need of investigation,
but rather uses the defined and referred pupil as the legitimate problem
with which he must deal. An interactionist educational psychologist
could not see the referral as something to be taken for granted, to be
accepted at face value. Rather, the process of social construction of
the pupil as a problem in need of referral and treatment is itself an
inherent part of the deviance and thus something to be investigated and
elucidated. To judge from the literature such an enterprise has held
little interest for educational psychologists. Research expenditure is
always a good index of interest; research into the labelling process in
schools is a minute fraction of research into the labelled product.

The deviant has been labelled already before he ever reaches the educational psychologist. Referral may constitute the first step of the *official*

process of deviance definition, but behind this lies the unofficial labelling process which in many cases has passed through a complex career lasting several years. It is to this topic that my own recent research (Hargreaves, Hester and Mellor, 1975) was in part directed. This shows that some pupils are typified by teachers as stabilised deviants as a product of extremely complex social processes within the school. Significantly most of these pupils who are deviants in the teachers' eyes never get referred to the psychologist; their deviant career never acquires any official status at all, though it is none the less real for that. Yet the teachers constantly invoke psychological vocabularies and psychological explanations to account for these pupils and justify their treatment of them. Teacher educators have made psychology and child development a central element in the curriculum of student teachers. It is hardly surprising that they pick up the vocabulary of their mentors, who have failed utterly to track the impact of what they teach on ordinary classroom teachers: I suspect that they would be rather horrified if they did.

I emphasise that most school deviants — the 'pests' and 'nuisances' and 'troublemakers' who for whatever reasons are not referred — are never seen by the educational psychologist at all, just as most young persons who break the law never reach the courts and become officially defined as juvenile delinquents. Of the pupils that the school defines and labels as deviant, that tiny minority of pupils who are referred to the educational psychologist are already at the final stage of the unofficial labelling process. Indeed, they do not reach the first stage of the official process until they are, in the school's eyes, fully-fledged deviants. Can the educational psychologist focus so exclusively on the labelled product that he can afford to ignore the process by which the teachers have come to define the pupil as so exceptionally deviant that he is in need of referral? Can he also ignore the process through which at the same time the pupil may have come to define himself as deviant? Can he ignore the fact that the pupil may interpret the fact of this (and each succeeding) interview with the educational psychologist as yet further confirmation that he is 'disturbed' or 'different' in some pejorative sense? Does the referral process, in the eyes of the pupil, constitute a transformation from being a mere 'troublemaker' (that is, someone who makes trouble for teachers, even if he does it rather more frequently than most) to being a 'case' in both official as well as popular meanings of that term (that is, someone who is 'sick' and in need of psychological/psychiatric help)? Just how stigmatising for the pupil is the process of referral?

It is only the tip of the iceberg of school deviance that comes into the view of the educational psychologist. Situated in a central clinic away from the school and overwhelmed by a heavy case load, he has little time to look under the surface of the water at what lies beneath, where the foundations of the referral process lie. But after the referral and the official process commences, he does have a critical decision to make about whether or not the pupil should take any further steps in the official deviant career. If he does accept the referred deviant, then he reaffirms the legitimacy of the teacher labelling and the referral process. He is in effect telling the teachers that they are right in defining the pupil as deviant and right in referring him to the psychologist for attention. The teachers' conceptions of deviance are confirmed and the processes that operate in the hidden parts of the iceberg are by implication supported. If the psychologist does challenge the referral — as he certainly does on occasion — then he effectively ends the official deviant career but merely returns him to the unofficial deviant career which led to the referral. When a psychologist sends a pupil back to the school 'untreated', then the teachers do not respond as the educational psychologist might wish, that is, by having to reconstruct their own definitions of deviance. Rather, the teachers simply counter-challenge the official definitions and the psychologist's legitimacy and competence to make definitions. The psychologist may send back the pupil as 'normal' but the teachers can reassert their own definitions on the grounds that 'everybody knows this kid is maladjusted' and that 'psychologists are fools'. The official deviant career is terminated, but the unofficial deviant career persists.

My own research interest has been in the area of unofficial labelling processes, whereas most of the labelling theory literature has been concerned with official labelling. Cicourel's (1968) major work on the labelling of juvenile delinquents is an excellent example of this literature which is of potential interest to educational psychologists. An important part of the interactionist perspective for educational psychologists would be the investigation of the official labelling process of school deviants as effected by the educational psychologists themselves. Their own contribution to labelling urgently needs to be examined. I know of only one major research in this area, namely Jane Mercer's work (1973) on the labelling of the mentally retarded. Here, one might be tempted to assume, we are on much firmer grounds with more objective criteria than in the case of a concept as vague as 'maladjustment'. However, Mercer points to a complex social process at the heart of the psychologists' work which does not reflect the conceptions of teachers who refer certain pupils to them. Mercer concludes:

> We found that becoming a mental retardate in the public schools is a
> complex social process which hinges on a series of crucial decisions
> made by teachers, principals, and psychologists. Some children are
> exposed to a much higher risk of achieving the status of mental
> retardate than others. The higher proportion of children from lower
> socioeconomic levels and minority groups in special education does
> not appear to be the result of higher overall rates of referral by
> teachers or higher rates of testing. Rather, it appears to be the result
> of the clinical diagnosis itself, a diagnosis that relies almost exclus-
> ively on an IQ test. Those who failed the IQ test were dispropor-
> tionately from lower socioeconomic groups and ethnic minority
> groups. Children recommended for placement and those actually
> placed were even more disproportionately from ethnic minorities
> and lower socioeconomic levels. Children whose backgrounds do not
> conform to the modal sociocultural configuration of the community
> are exposed to a higher risk of being labelled mentally retarded.

In other words, Mercer shows that mental retardation is not simply a
'fact' about certain persons which can be established by 'objective'
methods administered by any competent person; rather, whether or not
a person becomes labelled as a mental retardate hinges upon what kind
of psychologist is examining what kind of person with what kinds of
methods and procedures. The research indicates the urgency of the
need to examine the labelling of persons with much more diffuse categories such as 'maladjusted'.

The implications of the interactionist perspective on deviance for
educational psychologists are profound. Perhaps the most important is
that the psychologist should spend a substantial proportion of his time
in schools. With that change in location goes an equally significant
change in role, which is much more difficult to achieve, since teachers
will almost certainly expect the psychologist who is now 'on the
premises' to execute his traditional role as they define it — as tester and
psychotherapist. He would be under pressure simply to mop up teacher-
defined problems — and would be damned if and when he failed to do
so. A significant feature of the role change is an emphasis on *preventive*
work, so badly neglected in conventional role definitions, for if the
psychologist is present in school he can get access to and intervene in
the unofficial processes of labelling through which deviant pupils'
careers are generated. The rest of my remarks are devoted to illustra-

tions of the new tasks and opportunities that could become available through such a role change.

A central strand in interactionist theory is the commitment to what David Matza (1969) calls the 'appreciative' stance: the willingness to make an empathetic understanding and faithful exposition of the deviant's perspective on himself, his acts, his relations with others, his world. Too easily we all, social scientists included, assume that the official or labeller's perspective is the only valid or correct one. But if we listen to the deviant there are some surprises in store.

There is now massive evidence, both from academic research and from writers such as John Holt, that teachers have a very partial and selective understanding of pupils. They believe that they understand their pupils, so they constantly underestimate the wide range of thoughts, feelings, ideas and acts which pupils systematically hide from them. The educational psychologist in a school is in an excellent position to get access to the pupils' worlds and to relay them in the form of feedback to the staff. He would become an applied participant-observer. His job would not be to romanticise or to condone what he finds, but to expose it. Doubtless it would be a delicate and dangerous role, but it has enormous potential for changing and enlarging teachers' understanding of pupils and their treatment of them. One wonders, for instance, whether Werthman's (1963) spectacular material on delinquents in school could not, if used as feedback, have induced teachers to change their behaviour and thus reduce the frequency of misconduct. For Werthman's study, like many in the field, shows that delinquents' misbehaviour in class has a rational basis: it is an attempt to subvert the teacher's authority because the delinquents believe that the teacher is exercising his authority illegitimately. Until the teacher learns of the rational basis for the conduct, he will persist in his belief that it springs from malicious intent, defective personality, poor home background, or (by that popular but perverse tautology) from the fact that he is delinquent. Interactionist theory makes the working hypothesis that much school deviance, from minor classroom misbehaviour to serious truancy and delinquency, has a hidden rational basis. If the educational psychologist can reveal the hidden rationality, then traditional deviant labels would be questioned, interpersonal understanding and communication improved, and with luck appropriate adjustments in teacher conduct might change the situation to which pupil misconduct was a rational response.

Clearly this new role for the educational psychologist has an overt political dimension. There has always been a covert political element,

for when the clinic-based psychologist accepts a pupil on the grounds
that he is a truant or is maladjusted, he is in effect accepting the legitimacy of the rules which these pupils are breaking, the legitimacy of
those in power (teachers) to define such pupils as deviants in need of
treatment, and the legitimacy of the process of referral. He may prefer
to think of himself in more humanistic terms, as one committed to
individuals and their health and happiness, but what from his point of
view is individual amelioration (e.g. therapy) is from a wider perspective
a form of social control. In this sense the educational psychologist can
be described as a tool of the state, an upholder of the *status quo*. In the
change of role I am advocating, this political aspect becomes more
explicit and so more problematic.

   If an educational psychologist is to become involved in the school
itself, he must recognise that the school is a political system. The great
sociologist Waller (1932) knew this when he described the school as 'a
despotism in a state of perilous equilibrium'. If the psychologist parti-
cipates in that system, he will get his hands dirty, and his own political
allegiances and skills will immediately become relevant. Interactionist
theory looks at deviance in terms of interpersonal encounters and the
prevailing distribution of power in which those relations are embedded.
There is now suggestive evidence (Power *et al.*, 1967; Hargreaves, 1967,
1971; Reynolds, 1976, 1977) that both school organisation and the
content and means of enforcing school rules may be associated with
high rates of pupil deviance and delinquency. An adequate approach to
preventive work must include not only the individual level, where the
psychologist is most happy to work, but also the interpersonal and
institutional levels. If the school-based psychologist is to realise the
potential inherent in this innovation it is necessary for him to become
more informed of the relevant social-psychological and sociological
theory and research. In the clinic he can afford to ignore or underplay
the interpersonal and institutional aspects: in the school he must work
at all three levels.

   Interactionist writing has implications at all three levels and the
psychologist must be willing to apply them all. Some aspects of individual change can be mediated only through change at the institutional
level, and that fact can be avoided by claiming an allegiance to psychology. The psychologist who applies interactionist theory to the school
will soon find himself making some applications at the institutional
level where, it must be said, the school staff is most likely to be
resistant to innovation and change. The challenge is a daunting one but
educational psychologists are perhaps in the best position to respond to

it. For educational sociologists are currently in a state of deep
pessimism about interventionist work, are more likely to write
rhetorical tracts about the need for a major socialist revolution than to
enter the field in applied roles, and are deeply suspicious of psychologists and any work at the individual level. They have left the field open
to the psychologists.

The heart of the interactionist theory is nevertheless at the interpersonal level and offers considerable scope for an applied psychology.
Labelling theory does not assert, as some popular distortions allege,
that all deviant acts are caused by labelling. Usually a deviant act is
committed prior to its labelling or definition as deviant, so the labelling
cannot be said to cause the act. Generally interactionists have been
indifferent to the causes of the act prior to its definition as deviant,
which exposes one of the limitations of the theory. But labelling
theorists, following Lemert (1967), point out that once the labelling has
taken place, it becomes an inherent part of the phenomenon and that
under certain conditions the labelling may create problems for the
offender which may lead him to define himself as deviant (self-labelling)
and to indulge in further deviant acts as a means of resolving some of
the problems created by the deviance. For example, the labelling of
pupil misconduct as deviant may create a problem for the pupil, such
as resentment or hostility towards the teacher, which then becomes the
motive for further deviant conduct, either a repetition of the original
act (for new motives) or new forms of deviant conduct, such as physical
or verbal aggression towards the labeller. In that sense the labelling can
transform and exacerbate the deviance. Tannenbaum (1938) tended to
the view that all labelling was mischievous in that it creates self-
fulfilling prophecies which increase deviance and that the way out is to
refuse to dramatise evil by saying as little about it as possible. Schur
(1973) calls this a policy of radical non-intervention and his slogan is:
leave kids alone wherever possible.

It is dangerous advice. For we are torn between two truths. On the
one hand we know that the labelling of an act as deviant can in some
circumstances effectively inhibit the commission of further deviance. On
the other hand we also know, with the help of labelling theory, that the
labelling can in some circumstances exacerbate the deviance. The
problem is that we cannot specify precisely the 'in some circumstances'
of either claim. The research conducted by myself and my colleagues
confirms that it is not the intention of the labeller that matters, but
rather the content and manner of the labelling. The amplification of
deviance may be reduced if it is the *act* rather than the *person* which is

labelled. Our language permits us to define acts as deviant (e.g. theft, lie) without necessarily defining the person as deviant (e.g. thief, liar). Teachers regularly do both in classrooms and do not consciously differentiate between them or attach any significance to the difference. It may be that the separation of the act from the person is crucial, for only then can the labeller indicate to the offender that his acts are discrepant with his self and thus provide him with the opportunity for interpreting his act as inconsistent with both his self-concept and the identity that the labeller imputes to him. In driving a wedge between the (deviant) act and the (non-deviant) person, the labeller tries to ensure that the problem created by the labelling is one which is best solved by eschewing future deviant conduct. To label the person, not the act, as deviant is to inhibit the means by which the offender can create such a dissociation from his acts; instead the labelling denigrates him as a person, thus suggesting that his acts are in line with his (deviant) identity and giving him problems which can reasonably be solved by further deviance.

Many of teachers' deviant categories — like those of the traditional vocabulary of the educational psychologist — are categories of person (subnormal, truant, maladjusted, pest, troublemaker, etc.) not categories of act. The educational psychologist working in the school can undertake the essential research to test out ideas such as this as well as helping teachers to develop strategies and skills which may inhibit the acquisition of deviant identities by pupils. Educational psychologists have an impressive history of applying theory in ways that can be directly useful to teachers — one thinks of behaviour modification and microteaching — and interactionist approaches to deviance are rich in unexplored possibilities.

In this chapter I have offered a sketch of one interesting theoretical approach to deviance, which challenges many of the assumptions traditionally made by educational psychologists. Any useful applications of this perspective by educational psychologists would require a fundamental reappraisal of their role in relation to schools. It is evident from other chapters in this book that both kinds of re-orientation are in fact taking place. The interactionist approach to deviance can be used as one strand in, and as a general encouragement to, that wider reconstruction in educational psychology. If the applications of labelling theory are currently no more than suggestive, tentative and exploratory, then that is appropriate to a process of reconstruction, which is founded on an awareness of new horizons and a willingness to journey towards them.

6 THE FAILURE OF PSYCHOMETRICS

Bill Gillham

In the late seventies few psychologists give an intelligence test without a sense of unease, without a note of apology (or defensiveness) as if engaging in some shameful act. This is a most remarkable change and comparatively recent as a widespread phenomenon. Although partly a response to the *Zeitgeist* of liberal prejudice it is mainly due to an increasing awareness amongst psychologists of the conceptual and practical limitations of traditional tests.

The arguments against the utility of intelligence tests have been around for a long time. Simon's *Intelligence Testing and the Comprehensive School* was published in 1953 and, after twenty-five years, is still the best critique of psychometric concepts of intelligence. During the ensuing decade a number of important papers and books were published dismissing notions which had endured since the days of Lewis Terman — intelligence as 'capacity', intelligence as distinct from 'attainments', intelligence as a stable and relatively unteachable quality (Pidgeon and Yates, 1956; Vernon, 1958; Crane, 1959; Liverant, 1960; Hunt, 1961).

Yet for a long time the practice of intelligence testing seemed little affected by these criticisms — one manifestation of the durability of powerful, simple and easily communicated ideas. As late as 1965 Holtzman, writing about the concept of intelligence, could say that 'one of the most significant accomplishments of psychology has been the development of tests for measuring intelligence' (Brim *et al.,* 1966). Finishing my training as an educational psychologist in that year I am sure that I would have agreed with Holtzman. I can certainly remember being pleased to hear that a large-scale project was being set up at the University of Manchester to develop a *British* Intelligence Scale. I also remember hoping, vaguely, that it wouldn't be too different from the Stanford-Binet which I had administered something like a hundred times during my one-year training course.

I had been taught that the Stanford-Binet was a 'structured interview' — but it was a structure imposed on every child I interviewed; and I had been taught that, in Burt's phrase, 'tests . . . can still be but the beginning, never the end, of the examination of the child' — but they were always the beginning. Having spent a day a week practising the use

of tests I found them familiar and, indeed, reassuring: it was the reassurance of simplification — no matter what the situation I always had a
secure and well-rehearsed way of going about things. And since I had
learnt to 'interpret' a child's responses I could resist any doubts that I
might not be facing up to the real complexity of the child's approach to
the test problems. It was a self-maintaining system because, as I have
recently written elsewhere (Gillham, 1978) 'To become aware of this
complexity . . . one has to probe for it, otherwise it is possible to see
test responses as being simpler and more unitary than they really are;
and . . . to remain in ignorance of the psychological processes that are
actually involved.' But the very nature of the standardised procedure
and instructions of conventional tests prevented such explorations, and
this standardisation was sacrosanct. I can recall long discussions as to
the propriety of changing just *one word* in the Stanford-Binet
instructions; a similar change in the Book of Common Prayer could not
have excited more debate.

Personal reminiscences and reflections, even if they relate to experiences shared by the reader, may seem out of place in an evaluation of
psychometrics. But if psychology is our subject, then we are ourselves
part of our subject-matter; one of the neglected aspects of the debate
about the use and meaning of tests is their use and meaning to testers —
in other words the *psychology of test-giving behaviour.* If we were
conscious of the evidence and the arguments against traditional mental
testing practice and theory, why was it so long before we were affected
by them? Perhaps the answer is to apply psychological understanding to
ourselves. We don't expect other people to change their behaviour
simply by a process of intellectual conviction; and when patterns of
behaviour persist in the face of what seem to be very powerful arguments
we look for other kinds of psychological investment, and how these are
consolidated by the structure of social institutions.

For those psychologists brought up in the tradition of the
intelligence test as a basic part of every psychological appraisal — and
that is most of us — to stop this routine practice has meant dispensing
with a familiar and convenient frame of reference. The consequent
sense of insecurity is enhanced by the fact that there is nothing quite so
handy to replace it, either conceptually or practically: this has been the
main sticking point and we are none of us safely past it. Such practical
difficulties are, I suggest, the reason for the protracted time-scale of
change rather than reactionary tendencies or strong hereditarian beliefs.
But the trend is clear and even those psychologists who might regard
themselves as relatively traditional on testing matters are doing a great

deal less testing than they used to, or are testing for different reasons.

These changes within the profession have highlighted the social psychology of testing behaviour – the institutional processes which have served to keep us in our place. In our working life we are to some extent controlled by the tacit assumptions and expectations of other people; for the psychologist trying to get out of the testing role the irony is to realise that he has himself been responsible for determining such restrictive attitudes. Although 'imperialist' psychiatry may have been happy to keep psychologists as testers, it was psychologists who forged this identity in the first place. Having stopped teachers from giving intelligence tests (although Terman said they should), having for many years fought (and won) the battle to stop medical officers giving Stanford-Binets, psychologists are now saying that they don't want to do them and that they were mistaken about their usefulness. Yet relinquishing the commitment is not proving to be all that easy, since we have imbued parents, teachers, administrators and so on, with expectations about the value of tests and the psychologist's special role in giving them, and have created an institutional appetite for IQs. So although, in truth, psychologists are being constrained by others to do things they may not want to do, we need to be clear that these expectations are a result of what has been habitually observed of our past professional behaviour. And if we are to change such expectations effectively we must communicate something different by our present behaviour – by changes in our observed practice and not just by what we say.

This chapter is not intended as a diatribe against intelligence tests, nor as a critical account of psychometric concepts of intelligence: I have dealt with these elsewhere (Gillham, 1974, 1975) and the arguments need not be repeated here. My present concern is to consider the changing place of psychometrics as far as the role of educational psychologists is concerned. Why is it that psychologists no longer find it so useful to give individual, norm-referenced tests of hypothetical constructs? Personality tests make a good starting point for answering this question.

The virtual demise of personality testing in practice has attracted less attention than it might for there are lessons to be learnt from it. Apart from a few adherents amongst those trained to believe in the interpretive powers of psychologists, personality testing has never been a strong growth amongst educational psychologists in this country which is perhaps why it has not been missed. Over-represented in textbooks and on training courses it is interesting to note that the latter have been slow to catch up on changes in professional practice. At Nottingham University the course on personality testing was discontinued only four years ago; at about the same time University College London dropped its long-standing Rorschach course.

Both personality and intelligence tests have failed conceptually in terms of the assumptions that initially led to their widespread development; unlike intelligence tests, however, personality tests have also proved an empirical failure. A child who gets a low score on a comprehensive intelligence test is quite likely to have difficulty in coping with the school curriculum; a child who gets a deviant or abnormal score or interpretation on a personality test is not particularly likely to have conspicuous behavioural or emotional problems in his everyday situations. Such findings have been extensively reviewed by competent psychologists (Vernon, 1964; Mischel, 1968). Of course, the children who are usually given individual intelligence and personality tests are those who have already proved to have learning problems or who are seen as having emotional/social difficulties. The selected and pre-identified clinical group does not pose the threat of criterial validity, even if it does raise the question of the utility of confirming what is already known.

Mischel, noting that cognitive performance is more stable across situations than emotional/social behaviours, also observes that intelligence tests, whilst presuming to measure underlying traits like personality tests, do in fact sample the criterial *behaviours* to some extent — albeit in a one-to-one situation. It is worth noting here, since it has implications for what will be discussed later in this chapter, that tests of 'intelligence' correlate with school performance criteria to the extent that the test items sample academic performance (Vernon, 1960).

No personality test can be said to sample criterial behaviour (although some might claim to arouse something like real-life emotional states and attitudes). Rather such tests presume, either by responses to questions or to more or less structured 'projective' material, to sample underlying *traits* or *dispositions* of considerable generality across situations and relationships. The empirically demonstrated success of such statements of generality is crucial to the acceptability of personality trait theory and the use of personality tests: such evidence is manifestly lacking. Jensen (1964) reviewing the data on the validity of the Rorschach observes that its continued use tells us more about the psychology of credulity than anything else.

Mischel comments that

confronted by results of this kind, many clinicians have become
increasingly disillusioned with personality tests . . . [but] they often
still use and rely on techniques like the Rorschach and the TAT,
claiming that they employ them more as an interview than as a
standardised test . . . The justifiability of this practice depends, however, on the evidence supporting the value of clinical inferences and
judgements about dispositions from indirect behavioural signs . . .

Mischel points out that the data on such 'informal' uses are negative. It
is not enough to abandon or adapt invalid techniques; it is also necessary to abandon invalid ways of thinking.

But doubts about trait theory alone would not account for changes
in practice. More important, particularly in the case of the 'personality'
test, has been an increasing awareness of the social psychology of test-
giving behaviour, of what the psychologist is communicating (to the
child and others) by the act of giving a test — especially when the test
content is mysterious or ambiguous. Personality tests used with children
are most commonly of this type — for example, the Rorschach and the
Children's Apperception Test: in these instances the simplest message is
that the psychologist is finding out *what is wrong with the child,*
something deep and inaccessible to ordinary people by ordinary means
and so dependent on the psychologist's expertise and special instruments. Such a role has come to be seen by many as not only distasteful
but positively obstructive to establishing a helping relationship.

In the area of 'personality' problems, quite apart from the lessons to
be learned from social interaction theories of 'deviance', we have come
to recognise that a preoccupation with the aetiology of 'causes' of an
individual's difficulties is simply not *useful.* Our form of 'explanation'
needs to indicate remedial action. It is, in any case, doubtful whether
we can ever really explain or identify the causes of behaviour, although
many of us can contrive a plausible fiction that fits the evidence. What
we can do more usefully is to indicate possible changes in those factors
that might influence the 'problem' behaviour. In other words we
always need to construe the child's personality in social terms, in terms
of the effects on him of particular relationships and situations. There is
plenty of evidence to suggest that for the great majority of children
such a perspective makes the best sense.

It is a familiar experience as an educational psychologist to find that
a child's emotional 'disturbance' or 'disorder' disappears dramatically if
we change his situation — different class, different school, different
teacher, different work programme, admission to a hostel or special

school. Rutter *et al.* (1970) found that when parents and teachers were asked to identify the presence or absence of certain problem behaviours they each identified about the same number of children *but by and large they selected different children*. The correlation between parents and teachers ratings was negligible — +0.18. Interestingly enough such data did not prevent Rutter and his colleagues from subjecting the children screened out in this fashion to direct and indirect psychiatric appraisal to decide which of them had a 'clinically significant psychiatric disorder' — a very neat example of the difference between medical and psychological conceptions of emotional and behavioural problems. Personality tests are clearly part of the medical conception of 'intra-psychic' disorders. Their main use, in fact, has been to corroborate or clarify the psychiatrist's intuitive 'clinical' diagnosis. In other words apart from determining supposedly basic personality traits the tests have had a diagnostic function — to confirm that a child is suffering from a disorder of a certain kind.

For the practitioner, test validity, first and foremost, must be in terms of the *utility of what the test enables him to do.* Personality tests have often been used as an element in selecting children for child guidance treatment. Their validity in this instance would be demon-strated if children selected for such treatment by the use of personality tests were shown to derive more benefit than children not so selected. Such evidence is unlikely to be forthcoming, bearing in mind what we know about the predictive validity of personality tests on the one hand and the effectiveness of child guidance treatment on the other. The available evidence (Levitt, 1971; Shepherd *et al.*, 1971) indicates that there is no difference in outcome between children with difficulties who do, or do not, receive or accept 'treatment'.

Remedial action that goes beyond the narrow conception of clinical treatment involves asking the question — on a broad front — what factors need to be manipulated to modify a child's difficulties? This *social* perspective does not deny that some children have emotional/social problems of a highly transferable kind — across different relation-ships and different situations and different people's perceptions. Certainly some children, more than others, are locked into a way of seeing the world, a way of behaving that creates very general problems for them and for other people. It does not alter the fact that any change is going to come about through the modifying influence of social and interpersonal experiences. I have argued in Chapter 1 that as psycholo-gists we need to give priority to what are likely to be enduring difficul-ties for children. In the case of emotional and social problems this is primarily anti-social behaviour of a pervasive kind — and because it is pervasive there are more contexts maintaining it, more opportunities for the child to experience the punitive or ambivalent responses of peers and adults. The durability (and outcome) of such behaviour is not so much a function of 'psychopathic traits' in the individual concerned but of a self-maintaining interaction. True the child's 'constructs' may need modifying as part of the process of change but this can only be done by changing his social experiences so as to disconfirm them. Traditional personality testing has no place here: the problem exists not within people but between them, and not in the past but in the present.

Whilst empirical evidence can discredit a theory, it can never prove it. The relative success of intelligence tests as predictors is no proof of the existence of ability traits. In any case the correlation with criteria has never, with rare exceptions, been other than modest — usually around +0.5 to +0.7 (Cronbach, 1970). Terman's (1917) original claims for intelligence tests were based on a correlation with school subjects of +0.45 — about a 20 per cent relationship — which was none the less sufficient for him to advocate streaming by mental age. The much quoted data collated by Bloom (1964) relating to the stability of 'intelligence' (50 per cent of intelligence fixed by the age of five years) is based on the 50 per cent *relationship* (not amount) between intelligence test scores at five years and seventeen years. But such data derive from tests that were constructed on the *a priori* assumption that IQ was stable (Kaye, 1973). That is, a good intelligence test item was a 'stable' item — hence the central importance of the notion of item and test 'reliability'.

Inferences about 'intelligence' and 'ability' essentially derive from a child's progress in those culturally valued attainments which we distinguish as 'cognitive'. In our schooled society these relate to performance in the use of written and spoken language, the handling of spatial and numerical problems and, as a qualitative characteristic, the level of reasoning and categorisation displayed in all of them. When a child is described as having 'low intelligence' this means that he is not performing at his age-level in some, or perhaps all, of these important attainments. Our intelligence tests comprise a cursory sampling of these mixed up with items that are there for primarily psychometric (rather than psychological) reasons. But a low score on an intelligence test is usually seen as some kind of explanation, as some sort of inference from performance. Teachers commonly infer 'low intelligence' because a child cannot read and are usually heavily criticised for doing so. Of course they are wrong when they assume that the child who is a poor reader is necessarily going to be poor in other attainment areas, but in one important respect they are right: being 'intelligent' in our society includes being literate. Indeed, Olson (1975) argues that our kind of intelligence is heavily dependent on the structure of written language. By invoking a Rylian ghost to explain the workings of the machine teachers are doing no more than psychologists who use intelligence tests for the same purpose.

To some extent, and in so far as intelligence tests sample it, a child's present 'cognitive repertoire', to use Staats' (1968) phrase, does constrain what the child can go on to do. A child of ten who obtains a mental age of six years on the Stanford-Binet is almost certain to have difficulty in coping with the same curriculum as his contemporaries. But it does not explain why his reading level is low: so far as 'explanations' are useful both the 'mental age' and the 'reading age' require to be explained. Except in extreme instances all that the tests of hypothetical ability traits (like 'intelligence' or 'verbal ability') produce is a moderate probability statement about whether a child is likely to have learning difficulties.

When parents or teachers consult us about a child's learning problems they may well be interested to hear whether we agree that difficulties do exist; they will probably be interested to hear our speculations as to why the difficulties exist; *but they will be most interested to know what should be done to help the child and how it can be achieved.* Intelligence tests provide no help in this respect.

Intelligence testing may be out of vogue now and explanations in terms of 'innate general cognitive ability' unacceptable, yet we still have a number of more or less widely used tests that looked modern ten years ago because they purported to give a 'profile analysis' of skills and processes presumed to underly important areas of attainment. Although appealing to a slightly more sophisticated generation, these 'profile' tests can now be seen as the conceptual bedfellows of tests of 'intelligence'. For, in the same way, they professed to measure latent 'ability' or 'skill' constructs and so to explain or account for learning failure. However, constructs such as 'visual-perceptual ability' or 'psycholinguistic ability' or 'sequencing ability' are no better than the construct of 'intellectual ability' and, indeed, lack some of its psychometric virtues. I have in mind particularly tests such as the Illinois Test of Psycholinguistic Abilities and the Frostig Test of Visual Perception which profess, by the use of sub-tests, to sample key aspects of functioning underlying written and spoken language and to identify deficits in need of remediation. Whilst the ITPA does involve some language performance, neither test can be said to address itself directly or comprehensively to the behaviours of central concern. Both tests have been built from hypothetical constructs outwards and the items devised on the basis of these notions. This can be seen most clearly in the case of the ITPA.

I doubt whether Osgood's (1957) model of the language/communication process would be recalled other than by a few middle-aged experimental psychologists with long memories, if it had not been interred in Kirk's test. As far as I can understand it the model is an essentially formal one constructed of hypothetical variables, not intended to have comprehensive psychological reality, and certainly not intended to be assessed at each point of intersection which is what the ITPA claims to do. At the formal level Osgood's model has some appeal: there is something satisfying about its abstract tidiness. It is at the level of the test items constructed and assembled in its name that it becomes bewildering. Some sub-tests make more sense than others (although not particularly in terms of Osgood's model), but most of them make me feel like the reviewer of T.S. Eliot's *The Cocktail Party* who wrote that it must mean more than it appeared to but he couldn't see what it was.

It has been one of the distinctive characteristics of the professional psychologist and others like him that he has tended not to go direct to the actual problem. When the problem is reading failure in the classroom, the main of the psychologist's activity has been the ITPA and the Frostig in the Medical Inspection room and a 'diagnosis' in terms of deficits in 'visual closure', 'figure-ground discrimination', 'auditory sequencing' and the like. Explanations of this kind are as circular as using 'intelligence' tests to explain educational failure, with one important exception: we do not usually develop programmes to remedy deficits in intelligence. For one virtue of the tests I have been discussing is that they are referenced to activities of remediation (Kirk and Kirk, 1971; Karnes, 1968; Frostig and Horne, 1964); for this alone they have been important — their orientation was right even if their conceptual basis was faulty and their remediation activities of doubtful value.

Doing something over here to explain something over there via hypothetical constructs is a practical and conceptual hangover from days when the job was viewed more clinically and when psychologists were more concerned to differentiate themselves, in terms of their professional activities, from the laity. In place of complicated tests of ability and intelligence I suggest that we need to address ourselves directly to the attainments that are causing concern, and that it is important not to cloak our simple observations in the paramedical lan-

guage of learning 'disorders' or 'disabilities'. A former colleague once
remarked in my presence that a child was 'suffering from executive
aphasia'; in an inspired moment I suggested that what she meant was
that the child couldn't talk. Our statement needs to be in terms of what
a child can and cannot do in the attainment areas that matter, rather
than in the form of jargon that poses as explanation, particularly when
the 'diagnosis' comes via the circular route of inferred conditions and
hypothetical fictions. Quasi-medical terminology and 'specialised'
psychometry are the Emperor's clothes of the educational psychologist;
beneath the trappings of the test material and the jargon the psychologist really is naked, and in this state looks remarkably like anybody
else. Of course, this common identity could be used to advantage.

Educational psychologists, I suggested in Chapter 1, are employed
(and see themselves) as interventionists: their job is to initiate or bring
about change. It follows that the whole orientation of the assessment of
a child who is failing to learn must be *prospective* – in terms of what
the objectives should be and how they might be achieved, rather than
retrospective – in terms of quasi-explanatory cognitive deficits. In this
respect traditional 'attainment' tests have their uses; their weakness is
that although they tell you something about the present state of things
by taking some kind of performance sample, they tell you nothing
about what is maintaining this state of affairs and very little about
objectives or remediation. Yet a careful assessment of the *status quo*
comparing a child with his age-peers is a useful starting point; Binet
intended nothing more than this for his intelligence scale. If we had no
information about what a child could do then an intelligence test
(viewed as a grab sample of attainments) would at least alert us to
whether the child was, in Binet's term 'at age'; usually, of course, we
already know that the child is performing below his age-level so the
crude sampling of attainments represented by the intelligence test adds
little. In the case of the hypothetical child with no educational history,
norm-referenced tests of attainment in defined areas such as reading
comprehension or basic number skills would be a second level of investigation, but for most children they would be the first one.
  Norms are important because, in our culture, and particularly in
relation to children, the dimension of age-level is fundamental to our
perception of whether or not a problem exists. This is as true of emo-
tional-social behaviours (Shepherd *et al.*, op. cit.) as it is of school performance and that pre-school curriculum usually described as developmental milestones. The concept of age-norms does not preclude other
forms of reference such as a classification in terms of qualitative changes

since these are usually age-related. More important it does not preclude the use of criterion-referenced (i.e. content- or curriculum-referenced) forms of assessment. In fact they are mutually inclusive because the order and hierarchy of attainment objectives in an educational curriculum or programme reflects an age-progression, the psychological progression of learning development.

The norm-referenced test is only as good as its constructs or content. In other words a good attainment test must also be criterion-referenced in the sense of being an orderly sampling from a possible curriculum. A child's performance on such a test indicates two things, both relevant to action: how he compares with his age-peers, and roughly how far he has progressed in curriculum terms. It indicates priorities for further investigation and, to that extent, instructional objectives.

In practice, an assessment by an educational psychologist has tended to peter out just at the point where it could become useful. 'Attainment' tests, instead of being the beginning of an assessment for instruction, as they should be, have tended to round off an 'intellectual' assessment; further investigation and advice on instruction has usually been perfunctory, where it has occurred at all — and if teachers and parents are to be believed such occurrences have been rare. As I stressed earlier when referring to personality tests, for the practitioner test validity must be in terms of what it enables him to do. This is true of any form of psychological assessment: if it does not contribute to change it contributes nothing and the psychologist is wasting his time. If we are considering learning problems the essential requirements are these:

- accurate identification of those children whose level of attainment constitutes a handicap;
- an expanded (i.e. detailed curriculum-referenced) assessment to determine precisely what a child can and cannot do — that is, what a child needs to be taught and what he already knows;
- an investigation of how the child views or understands the learning tasks and of how instruction has been organised — not to identify 'causes', but to ascertain where the difficulties lie and what can be changed to improve learning performance;
- bearing in mind the objectives identified in the curriculum-
  referenced assessment, the more or less detailed specification of remedial procedures;
- determining criteria and methods for evaluating progress.

What is immediately obvious is that there is nothing here about 'disorder' or 'disability' or 'diagnosis': the constructs are those of the teacher and the educationalist rather than the psychological clinician. It does not involve the use of 'restricted' tests (or restricted constructs). Except in an advisory capacity it need not involve the psychologist at all. In other words a more valid form of assessment may involve the psychologist in less work.

The concern with the devolution of assessment has been a factor in the grass-roots expansion of screening procedures linked to remediation programmes – a movement of great promise, and significant for the future role of the educational psychologist. Its success depends upon how far it meets the five requirements set out above. An examination of the screening instruments produced in this country and the similar 'readiness' tests produced in the US shows that many of them would fail at the initial level of identification (Evans, 1975).

Whether applied at an individual or a group level (usually the latter) screening is basically a selection procedure in the first instance; identifying a minority group of children who are expected to have exceptional learning or behaviour problems. Apart from the defects in the construction of many recent screening measures (too short, or too vaguely worded or specified to be reliable let alone valid) some of them also assume that they can accurately predict 'pre-symptomatically', i.e. identify those children who will subsequently have difficulty, for example in learning to read, although at the time of the assessment they are 'pre-reading'.

Undoubtedly there are precursors to physical and psychological handicaps, what is doubtful is that we can accurately specify them. In educational psychology it has been widely assumed that we know the skills basic to reading and that these can be assessed, before reading itself actually appears, so that children who are likely to have difficulties can be given special attention. The study by de Hirsch, Jansky and Langford (1967) which reported a high level of predictive accuracy over a two-year period stimulated a lot of interest in this approach. But subsequent work including Jansky and de Hirsch's little-known followup (1971) produced disappointing results.

It is interesting to note that at a time when psychologists are coming to favour comprehensive screening procedures to identify 'at risk' children, the Court Report on medical services (HMSO, 1976) has recommended the abandonment of 'at risk' registers – official endorsement of a failure spanning fifteen years. The history of this is well summarised by Davie (1976) and it has clear implications for the current activities of educational psychologists. Davie refers to the influence of an article by Mary Sheridan (1962) published in the Monthly Bulletin of the then Ministry of Health:

> Sheridan, a gifted clinician, listed all of the factors which in some circumstances and having regard to the individual case, she considered might place a child at risk. Within a very short time risk registers were kept by most local health authorities and hopes were apparently high. However no research studies or operational evaluation had been carried out . . . Some health authorities . . . had slavishly listed virtually all of Sheridan's criteria on cards for each child born in their area . . . Other authorities pruned the list of risk factors but without any firm evidence to guide them. Finally, it was found that, overall, the proportion of children with defects or disabilities on the risk registers was disappointingly small and, conversely, an unacceptably large number of such children had been excluded from the registers.

The Croydon Screening Procedures (Wolfendale, 1976), which are well known, are of the pre-symptomatic kind in that the initial checklist samples behaviours which are presumed to precede or underlie later school performance: what are assumed to be relevant remediation activities are then specified. However, the procedures are characterised by an almost total lack of evaluative support. Wolfendale states: 'several Local Education Authorities are using the checklist and are less concerned with its validity as a predictive instrument than they are with its face validity for identifying children early on, as a precursor to action'. Medical 'at risk' registers had face validity too.

The best predictors of behaviour seem to be early forms of the behaviour in question: in curriculum terms, the first steps in the curriculum. You do not really know whether a child is going to have a speech problem until he starts to talk — or unless the start is very much delayed (and not always then). An intelligence test's ability to predict how well a child will answer questions at seven increases considerably when he becomes able to answer questions at two to three years of age. The best single index, pre-school, of whether a child will learn to read easily is whether or not he knows his letters (Downing and Thackray, 1971).

Test content that is based on a real (or possible) curriculum rather than psychologists' notions has a manifest validity which can obscure the need for technical adequacy. If assessment has become liberated from some of the old constraints it is none the less important that it retains those traditional psychometric virtues which are relevant to its purposes. Some content-referenced screening instruments, despite the virtue of going direct to the curriculum, take such a small sample or such an unsystematic one that they must fail to be reliable, which means they fail to predict. The critical requirement for an initial screening procedure is that it be short enough for large-scale administration yet long enough to take a reliable sample of the attainments in question, otherwise too many children will be selected for further, more detailed scrutiny to justify the time and effort that that requires. A fine-grain analysis of attainment is only justifiable if the initial screening is pretty accurate since it is only necessary with children who are having difficulty in making progress.

At the same time, anyone who has been involved in introducing criterion-referenced assessment into schools will know that the concept of a hierarchy of objectives which it entails has an impact on curriculum organisation in general. Such a spread effect is to be expected because assessment of the child who is failing, is also an appraisal of how well the school organises its teaching. In the past the assessment of children, particularly individual testing by the clinic-based psychologist, was not seen, in any sense, as an assessment of the school; curriculum-based assessment carried out primarily by teachers changes this. If part of the psychologist's job is to influence school organisation and curricular practice so that individual children's learning problems and social adjustment difficulties are diminished, then such a shift of responsibility for assessment is essential. Neither this nor participation in the development of remediation procedures renders the psychologist into a 'super teacher'; it is doubtful whether in all cases he would be able to do the job of the teacher he is helping. Teaching children and assessing their progress is the teacher's business: the psychologist's role is to help him define and attain his curriculum objectives particularly in respect of children who are failing.

Having expropriated testing activity psychologists now find that to do their job properly they have to hand it back. This means that they must also give up their expertise, such as it is. Attempts to retain control of local enterprise by the use of 'item banks' based on Rasch item scaling (Elliott, 1976) seem likely to fail as Goldstein and Blinkhorn (1977) have recently pointed out. Here, as previously in the history of psychometrics there is the danger of the constraint and interference of what Guttman (1971) calls 'a priori statistical considerations'. The concepts and techniques of psychometrics are valid only so far as they enable us to facilitate the process of educational and personal development in children: the failure of psychometrics has been the poverty of its contribution.

7 COMMUNITY PSYCHOLOGY

David Loxley

Although educational psychologists are a somewhat inconspicuous group, they do occupy a strategic vantage point in terms of surveillance of the social and educational scene. Their observations ought, theoretically, to be of value in facilitating the responsiveness of the education service to the community's needs, and in particular to the needs of the underprivileged. And yet it is arguable that educational psychologists exert comparatively little influence in this direction, and when they do, that this has often less to do with their actual relationship with the community than with an abstract professional opinion based on some pre-established normative criterion.

This raises the question of whether educational psychologists do, in fact, work on behalf of the community (their 'client' population) or whether they occupy the role of impersonal functionaries whose task is primarily to 'oil the wheels of the system'. If we are obliged to admit that the latter description is, in some ways, closer to the truth, it might be pertinent to consider why this is the case and whether it must inevitably be so.

It seems that the history of educational psychology to date has been dominated by two models. One is the nineteenth-century 'natural science' model by which psychology sought to establish its *scientific* respectability. This model is characterised by its *methodology* which is hypothetico-deductive and relies heavily on quantification and the replicability of its experimental data. The second model is complementary to the first and is characterised by the activities of *diagnosis* and *treatment,* i.e. the 'medical' model, by the adoption of which applied psychology sought to gain its *professional* respectability. The 'natural science' model is the more difficult to apply outside the laboratory but with the help of statistical methods the psychometrists were able to create an applied science of a kind. The child guidance clinics on the other hand, as the word 'clinic' implies, utilised the medical model, although their 'patients' were not usually ill.

The problem of both models is that they tend to create a Procrustean bed for the client; that is if indeed they recognise an individual client. For if a child is 'identified' by school or by survey as a 'problem', who is really the client? Was Burt's client, 'the backward child' or 'the young delinquent', or was it, in fact, the LCC? I think it is evident that it was the latter and that much intervention by psychologists today, whether LEA or school initiated, and directed at populations, groups or individual children, is of very much the same kind.

This is not necessarily a bad thing in itself since LEAs and schools exist for the purpose of acting in the interest of the child population. Nevertheless, there is undeniably the danger that the problem of the client organisation may be translated into the problem of the 'identified' child. Educational psychologists have had a tendency to conceptualise 'the problem' as within the child, rather than as a problem of interaction between the child and his surroundings, still less as a projection of an organisational problem manifested *through* the child. Well isn't it obvious that the problem of a mongol child, for example, is his mongolism? No, it isn't, because the problem exists not in his chromosomes but in the question of how to meet his needs. The school system really has the educational problem. Thus, diagnosis as 'ESN' has become stigmatic, for although 'educational subnormality' was intended to denote operational rather than qualitative criteria, in practice it is treated as a personal attribute. A natural corollary is that we tend not to expect the 'normal' system to meet the needs of a 'subnormal' individual.

If the medical model has made us overly concerned with the diagnosis of problems within individuals, the 'natural science' model, pursued with such unnatural zeal by psychologists, may have led us into believing too confidently in the accuracy of our diagnoses. Educational psychologists have become identified primarily as diagnosticians and their main diagnostic instrument is taken to be the psychometric test which represents almost the only evidence for the claim of the traditional educational psychologist to be a scientist. In fact the uncritical use of tests is really rather convincing evidence to the contrary. The inevitable reductionist formula frequently obscures rather than illuminates the actual phenomena with which the psychologist is supposedly concerned. It often replaces entirely the explication of complex meaningful events.

I recently saw a 'psychological report' which consisted of a set of IQ scores with one line of interpretation to the effect that, since the child's attainment exceeded his 'capacity' he should be transferred to the less demanding atmosphere of an ESN school. This extraordinary diagnosis bore no reference to the fact (obtained from another source) that the child concerned had just been uprooted from his home following the separation of his parents and had been placed with relatives in a distant town where his new school had instantly referred him for emotional difficulties.

It would seem that if we cannot stretch the child to fit the system's requirements we can at least reduce him to fit the limitations of our diagnostic categories! I think the above illustration demonstrates that this is not a caricature nor a serious exaggeration of the case. This kind of *reductio ad absurdum* results from the uncritical acceptance by the psychologist of *measurement* as the prerequisite of scientific enquiry.

Giorgi (1969) has argued eloquently against this misconception, pointing out that measurement is not in itself intrinsic to scientific methodology, but merely represents an appropriate approach to the explanation of the phenomena with which physical scientists are concerned. A conception of psychology as a *human* science would only rely on measurement in so far as it remained appropriate to do so, but to be true to its subject matter would need to rely on other methods also. Giorgi's preferred methodology for psychology as a human science is derived from phenomenology. Research, as he points out, does not necessarily entail experimentation nor quantification. Phenomenological research is concerned with the context, quality and meaning of phenomena. In the research setting, or in the clinical setting, the subject's or client's interpretation of events is crucial and the experimenter or therapist construes his own position as that of participant observer. Above all, phenomenological psychology attempts to be true to its data, and to avoid the reductionism to which the positivistic paradigm of 'natural science' psychology invariably tends. Of course, many educational psychologists are very aware of the risk of relegating the client to the status of a numerical formula. The growth in interest in personal construct theory amongst educational psychologists is a step in the direction of a phenomenological paradigm in that it attempts to illuminate the meaning of the client's experience.

The relevance of phenomenology to psychology in the community lies in its emphasis on the contextual. A community represents the shared life-space of its collective membership. The inhabitants of a neighbourhood or a street may be a community in that they share certain types of experience, e.g. of social class, education, income, etc. A school, hospital or work place population is a community in a further sense in that a more formal type of membership is shared: there are more formal and informal rules, rituals and signs of membership. Psychologists will only have a community emphasis in so far as their psychology has a community orientation. A phenomenological approach is appropriate in that it encourages participant observation. It does not exclude measurement as an element of data collection but the measurement process ceases to be central. The definition of 'behaviour settings' in the manner of ecological psychology (Barker, 1968) offers one systematic way of representing the community context.

Educational psychologists, however, appear to pay very little attention to the psychology of schools by contrast to the amount of attention they focus on individual children. This emphasis possibly owes as much to the 'medical model' as to the 'natural science' model. Educational psychologists sometimes refer to themselves as 'consultants', and have been known to equate the teacher with the 'GP'. Perhaps we should look more closely at this model and at the nature of professionalisation.

Illich's polemical critique of professional medicine, *Medical Nemesis* (Illich, 1975) is sub-titled 'The Expropriation of Health', which he amplifies as 'the expropriation of Man's coping ability by a maintenance service which keeps him geared up to the industrial system'. The concept of professionalisation as expropriation deserves consideration. Is it applicable to psychology? Since the subject matter of psychology rightfully belongs to everyone, it is certainly arguable that its translation into an area of 'professional expertise' does constitute such an expropriation. If psychologists represent themselves as experts in other people's affairs, while maintaining as a 'professional secret' the basis of their expertise, this formulation is confirmed. Of course it is not usually expressed in this way: the aspect of professional secrecy appears more by default than by design, in our not expressing the limitations of our skills and methods.

Illich has shown that the concept of a 'helping profession' is at least part myth. This is not to question the possibility of genuine altruism as a motive, but to raise the question of whether the helping professionals are not themselves mystified as to their role in the normative social order. Are they not, actually, agents of *social control*? 'Child guidance', after all, originated out of the intention to curb delinquency, and all forms of selection (e.g. for grammar schools or special schools) can be seen as ways of rationing scarce resources, without questioning why the resources are scarce.

Ingleby (1970) states 'Psychologists claim to be social engineers, but turn out to be really maintenance men: in this, perhaps, they are only sharing in the fond aspirations of all skilled mechanics.' He suggests that psychologists like to view their science as 'objective' and 'value free' when in fact their choice of models illustrates, by 'prediction' and 'control' and by 'diagnosis' and 'treatment' (in the absence of illness), the assertion of a standard set of values associated with the maintenance of order and the elimination of deviance. Some psychologists may see the latter as appropriate and desirable objectives. Eysenck for instance advocates a 'technology of consent' which he defines as 'a generally applicable method of inculcating suitable habits of socialised conduct into the citizens (and particularly the future citizens) of the country — or preferably the whole world' (Eysenck, 1969).

I do not think that to reject Eysenck's utopia is to advocate disorder and anarchy. Phenomenological and humanistic psychology tends to be more optimistic about 'human potential'. Its emphasis represents a shift from professional expropriation of control towards self-determination on the part of the client. Of course limits must be set to certain kinds of deviant behaviour, but the behaviour itself must be comprehended as meaningful rather than meaningless. The labelling process tends to obscure the meaning by reference to factors such as aggression and frustration as though they lacked intentionality (words like 'aimless' and 'meaningless' are often employed). But aggression is aimed at something (or how would we recognise it?) and frustration is frustration within a context. If we relate behaviour to its context in the experience of the subject we are adopting the 'appreciative' perspective (Matza, 1969) as opposed to the diagnostic/corrective perspective. By separating intentionality from causal determination we are not taking a stand on moral responsibility but facilitating awareness of the phenomenon *as perceived by the subject* rather than as interpreted by normative criteria of health or morality.

One outcome of the appreciative perspective in practice has been the recognition that both the punishment and treatment of young offenders are equally unsuccessful which has led Schur (1973) to advocate a policy of 'radical non-intervention'. Educational psychologists, however, appear to have an officious urge to intervene, even though they may themselves be sceptical of the benefits. It seems they have been trained to respond to crises, although they might feel they would be more fruitfully occupied in the area of prevention.

Preventive work itself however presents a further problem concerning evaluation. How can it be proved that anything has been prevented, and what, in any case, is to be prevented and on whose behalf? We are face to face, once again, with the question of who is the client? Are we preventing trouble for the school by the early detection and treatment or removal of deviants, or are we seeking to prevent distress and educational failure by means of an internal organisational response? If it is the latter, then we should be focusing our attention on the school rather than the child. We will be concerned with matters of curriculum and organisation, with rules, rituals, attitudes and values.

We have now accomplished a significant shift in emphasis: we are treating the school as a community which wishes to maximise the self-actualising potential of its members, rather than an institution with purely instrumental goals, which must be serviced and maintained. The evaluation of 'prevention' is therefore subordinate to the evaluation of our success in influencing the school towards the former (community) conception rather than the latter (factory) conception. Prevention becomes a consequence of *organisational* change.

Living is inseparable from learning, and it is a truism that the living and learning *environments* of human beings influence in a major way their capacity to live and learn effectively. If we tolerate the social reality of overcrowding, slum conditions and high-rise flats without play areas and with paper-thin walls, then we are ignoring the ecology of learning as much as any other aspect of the quality of life of those we permit to live in this way. It is bad faith in the extreme to pretend that we are not 'professionally' concerned, if we are, at the same time, willing to write elaborate psychological reports based on purely intra-psychic factors as though educational performance and emotional stability were entirely independent of their context. Surveys carried out by psychologists would be more honest and convincing if they high-lighted ecological variables. The trouble with many epidemiological studies is that they do not go far enough in the identification of environmental factors. The National Child Development Study is a praiseworthy exception which has certainly identified poverty as more widespread and damaging than many planners and politicians would like to believe.

Unfortunately we seem to have a sort of 'normal curve' mentality about this. While it is still held by some that the 'deserving poor' deserve *to be* poor, a more popular view is that poverty is a natural outcome of the downward social mobility (or upward immobility) of the inherently feckless or unintelligent. The 'cycle of deprivation' bandwagon, there-fore, is as attractive to advocates of draconian 'eugenic' measures as it is to the protagonists of social reform. It is possible that the influence of psychologists, to date, has given greater support to the former than to the latter, and, as long as educational and clinical psychologists are willing to wield IQ tests, this is likely to remain the case.

A reconstruction of the role of psychology in the community has been under way in the United States for more than a decade. The community psychology movement began in the 1960s. Its growth has

paralleled the recent acceleration of the community development
movement, which is also visible in this country, and with which it
shares much common ground. During the extremely turbulent period of
the sixties, when the ghettos and campuses of America seethed with
political activity, the watchword of shrewd government became 'participation'. The poverty programme, Project Headstart, and the
community mental health programmes were part of the American
administration's response to the politics of pluralism. The slogan of the
militants was 'Power to the people'. Psychology, both academic and
applied, underwent its own related vicissitudes. Activists within
psychology were supporting the civil rights campaigners who were
initiating successful legal action against streaming and segregated educational programmes which discriminated against blacks and other
minority groups on the basis of their selection by culturally biased
tests. The campaigners at state level were no doubt encouraged by
Senator Sam Ervin's chairing of a Senate Sub-Committee on Constit-
utional Rights, directed specifically at questioning the ethics of
psychological testing.

The undeniable success of the movement against testing in America
must have given many psychologists food for thought. There are those
in this country who believe that the security of tenure of educational
psychologists is assured by their quasi-statutory role in regard to assessment for special education. It is instructive to peruse the commentary
of the Community Relations Commission on the 1976 Race Relations
Act, issued to local authorities in March 1977, in which appeared the
following:

> The concept of indirect discrimination . . . may also be applicable to
> many aspects of education. For instance, unjustifiable selection or
> screening criteria might be discriminatory in effect . . . Similarly, the
> assessment of children for placement at ESN(M) schools which dis-
> proportionately affects certain groups may be contrary to the
> indirect discrimination provisions.

If admission to ESN school is likely to be considered discriminatory
against certain groups on racial grounds, it is obviously not regarded as
a privilege. In these circumstances it seems pointless to deny that there
is a stigma attached. In addition, the available research gives us little
grounds for optimism in relation to the efficacy of segregated education
for slow learners (Miller, 1973). In fact it is logically obvious, and the
psychological evidence bears it out that homogeneous groups of 'slow

learning' children are unlikely to provide a stimulating educational setting by reason of their composition, even if we discount the possible influence of the self-fulfilling prophecy.

The recognition of these facts has led some educational psychologists to be hesitant about recommending special school placements, preferring rather to work with teachers in the ordinary schools in the construction of individualised programmes. However, in some areas this has already produced conflict as numbers in ESN schools have declined and teachers have (understandably) felt threatened. The psychologist in this context, acting as client advocate, is undoubtedly out on a limb if also identified as *controlling* the admission procedure. This brings the question of identification of the real client into sharp relief. The psychologist may well believe that the child will progress at least as well in the ordinary school system as in the ESN school, and without the social consequences of stigma. But a head-teacher may disagree with the psychologist's recommendation because he believes he must defend the interest of the other children in his school from whom the 'slow learner' allegedly creates a disproportionate diversion of resources. The head may well believe himself to be the client, having 'commissioned' the psychologist, and that if he is not satisfied with the advice obtained, he should have the right to reject it. He may feel he is denied this right if the psychologist seems to over-rule his own opinion. The psychologist's own solution may well be treated as *unworkable* simply because it is, in effect, being forced on the school. In the absence of a change in policy (e.g. the redeployment of special and remedial resources) there may be no solution to this impasse.

Psychologists are much more likely to be able to exert a positive influence on behalf of children if they are free to pursue objectives of organisational change by means of persuasion backed by research evidence, but without seeming to pre-empt the process by unilateral action. *It follows that if educational psychologists are to have an independent advisory function they should not be implicated in formalised assessment procedures.*

The example of special education highlights an alternative function of educational psychologists which might best be described as research and evaluation. A psychological service could be the type of agency suggested by Downs (1967) which understands the main organisation but is 'detached enough to propose changes involving major departures from the *status quo*'. In connection with a school the objectives set might be curricular or organisational (Glaser, 1973), certainly applying cognitive developmental psychology in the manner suggested by Bruner

(1968) in order to 'organise knowledge to fit learning', and also looking at the school as a human community.

Psychologists should be concerned with the school as a *community within an organisation* in constant interaction with a larger *community within a social structure*. How are the personal needs of the client community met by these organisational and social structures? Of course this is the ground where psychology meets sociology. Psychologists gain a unique perspective on organisations from the vantage point of their work with individuals whom the organisations characterise as deviant, but this perspective requires both a psychological and a sociological framework if the situation is to be understood in a holistic way. Archibald (1976) has suggested that a *rapprochement* between the disciplines of psychology and sociology is long overdue. From our position 'in the field' we must surely agree.

Projects within organisations and in the community are often suggested by the needs of particular individuals. For educational psychologists curricular and organisational projects in schools might be built around the routine subject areas of literacy and numeracy, or extend into the area of the curriculum associated with health and social education, especially education for personal relationships. The development of resources for helping children with reading difficulties is a familiar field to educational psychologists and many also take an interest in the pastoral care structure of schools.

Accommodating children's special needs in the ordinary school system requires sensitive handling whether the special need is long term (as with congenital handicap) or arises suddenly and unexpectedly (e.g. a bereavement or a schoolgirl pregnancy). In the case of the pregnant schoolgirl, for instance, especially where termination of the pregnancy is not chosen or is left too late, what is the best way to help the girl both with her personal and educational needs? This raises many delicate issues, not least those arising from the attitudes of teachers, but there is some evidence that modification of attitudes can occur (Preston and Lindsay, 1976) and that once the defences of denial and rejection have been lowered, progress can be made towards humane and liberal solutions of problems which are *both* personal and organisational.

The tendency to reject (or eject) the deviant from the 'normal' system is an atavistic assertion of the old morality associated with foundling homes, workhouses and asylums. Denial is an unhealthy societal defence mechanism with which the psychological professions ought to be concerned. Educational psychologists have a primary role in helping educational institutions to become 'normal' communities by meeting the needs of a natural cross-section of the population, including the handicapped and the unfortunate. This obviously entails an inter-disciplinary exercise with teachers and others, to which one kind of input is the psychological explication of classroom problems (Galloway, 1976a) as well as work on the organisational implications of an inte-grationist policy.

Current research in Sheffield, concerned with the early identification of special needs by systematic observation in early education, seems to be revealing very few such needs which cannot be met by the ordinary schools, at least in the first two years (Lindsay, 1977). If this is the case, the implication is that 'early intervention' leading to transfer is much less appropriate than many people believe. Furthermore, it raises the question as to why some children who apparently make satisfactory progress, according to their teachers, at the infant/first school stage, do not maintain this progress. The argument which relates this to the 'capacity' of the child to cope with more complex learning tasks is seductive, if we ignore its essential circularity. The 'intelligence' test tells us no more than that the child who finds certain tasks difficult often finds certain other tasks difficult, and the more similar the tasks the closer the correlation. This is hardly astonishing information, but when followed by the logical *non sequitur* which relates this to an inherent limitation of intellectual potential requiring segregated educa-tional provision, it becomes immoral on two counts. First, the scientific foundations of such an assertion remain highly questionable in most cases, despite a century of the 'nature-nurture' controversy, and secondly, it begs the question of the responsibility of 'normal' institu-tions to meet a 'normal' cross-section of needs.

The mathematics of the 'normal curve' applied to explain educa-tional performance supplies the perfect justification for educational failure *on the part of the educators* by invalidating the right of an arbitrarily defined group to be considered 'normal' in the everyday sense. An alternative approach is expressed by Glaser (op. cit.) who, in discussing developing trends in educational psychology, states 'the assumption now is that ways can be found to ensure that most children will master the literacy objectives of elementary school, and the explicit tactic is to place the burden on the instruction to maximise the ways in which the child can progress rather than necessarily assuming that the child lacks a particular capability or aptitude'.

McClelland (1973) concludes a powerful assault on the validity of 'intelligence' testing by making a case for criterion sampling as a means of monitoring progress towards real life outcomes. There are strong

indications that 'criterion referenced testing' is already becoming the
vogue (Ward, 1975). Testing of this kind is inextricably bound up with
teaching for it represents the feed-back process which regulates input
and constitutes 'knowledge of results' to both teacher and learner.
Nevertheless, as a merely terminal or *post hoc* event the regulatory
effect of testing is seriously weakened. To assess progress in retrospect
may be as unhelpful to the learner as to assess 'potential' in advance: in
the former case needs may be recognised too late, as in the latter case
'capacity' is determined too soon.

In the case of normative testing of attainment both sins are frequently committed at once when the testing is part of a large-scale programme. The usual programme of this type is a reading survey which
provides no information as to why certain children are failing, but
rather tends to 'justify' the failure of a certain proportion of the
population by reference to the 'normal' distribution of scores. One reaction to the educational standards debate may be the introduction of
more of this kind of testing, in which case complacency will prevail. As
an experienced remedial teacher puts it 'the answer is not always to be
found in quotients, standard deviations or rituals which do not assist
good teaching in any way' (Edwards, 1972). I would go further and
suggest that 'the answer' is rarely to be found in this way and that for
psychologists seemingly to imply that it is, is to assert a spurious
expertise. This is not to say that statistical computation is never a useful
means of establishing 'the answer' in certain situations, but I think it
presumes a different question. This question is concerned with quality
('good teaching') not quantity. Thus a criterion referenced evaluation of
progress woven into the curriculum as a cumulative record would be a
way of systematising good teaching. This should be integrated with a
'branching programme' of curricular possibilities which takes account of
individual needs by means of alternative task structures. Applying
Bruner's approach to a theory of instruction, we should be concerned
with the growth of cognitive competence through the successive combination of simpler levels of competence into more complex performances.

While educational psychologists certainly have a role in the development and evaluation of educational programmes of this kind, it should
be emphasised that their implementation, including any implications for
assessing progress, would be a matter for teachers. The move to criterion referenced assessment should eventually mean that the psychologists as consultant educational diagnosticians *are no longer required*.
This is the proper outcome of what might be called the 'project to

improve the diagnostic resources of the teacher' in the appropriate context of the school. A psychological service geared up to research and
development projects should logically 'work itself out of a job', not
hypothetically 'come the millenium', but repeatedly. Projects should be
activities with a discernible beginning and end.

An emphasis on project-orientated work opens up many possibilities
in terms of targets and methods. Participant observation is an appropriate method for psychologists to enhance their knowledge of organisations and the community, for example by working temporarily in a
particular school, or working with the youth service (perhaps on an
informal detached worker basis) within a specified neighbourhood, or
becoming involved with a particular cultural or ethnic sub-group.
Working informally with adolescents and amongst ethnic minorities was
a characteristic of the activities of educational psychologists in Norwich
and in Huddersfield in the middle and late 1960s. In this way very much
more was learned about the experience and needs of the communities
concerned than clinical or psychometric operations were capable of
revealing. It would be naive to assert that a significant contribution to
human welfare or 'race relations' was made directly as a result of these
activities, but the experience was invaluable in terms of knowledge
gained and the operational principles which began to develop.

Educational psychologists are in a good position to be mediators in
some matters concerning community needs and public policy. This
does not mean that they should attempt to usurp the function of the
community's political representatives but that they should help the
client community to articulate its needs and the politicians to
interpret them in terms of policy. This role makes use of the psychologist's strategic position and enables psychological 'expertise' to be
offered in an understandable and assessable form as a particular interpretation of events which can be judged on its merits by the other
participants.

Whether the participative model is less 'expropriative' than the
model of professionalisation discussed earlier must in the end be
largely a function of how the individual psychologist makes use of the
participative role, as compared with the psychometric-diagnostician
role. A fair criticism might well be that the role in either case is inseparable from the personality of the actor, but it should be clear that
the models themselves presume different goals.

The consequences of labelling and the self-fulfilling prophecy are
obviously contentious moral issues which must be confronted as
possibilities of the medical model in practice. The participative model,

on the other hand, takes as problematic, not the question of 'diagnosis' but the nature of the relationships between people and within communities. It is concerned with the social phenomena of interaction, the implicit rules and symbols of social discourse. One works with a client, or possibly a number of clients, in meeting the demands of a particular situation, rather than working on a 'case' or problem individual. The community is the field in which the psychologist actually works, located physically by the neighbourhood (of which the home and the school are, for the educational psychologist, perhaps the most salient parts) and identified in human terms by its population (again salient groups being the school population and the family). The hospital, community-home or other care agency, of course, may also be the salient loci or mini-communities but the client is a person (or people) rather than an abstract organisation. The psychologist's function should be that of client advocate rather than that of organisational functionary. Working *with* people, the psychologist is a facilitator rather than a direct change agent; a participant observer with one interpretation of events to be considered in relation to others rather than an expert diagnostician or consultant. The 'expertise' involved is based solely on the psychologist's knowledge and/or experience of similar situations (as is that of the client), plus a range of channels of communication and sources of information and help.

This view repudiates much that is involved in the process of professionalisation. It does not represent the psychologist as having a special and professionally private range of skills which are totally distinguishable from those of a school counsellor, a social worker or a community worker. To be sure, the psychologist will tend towards a particular frame of reference, and experience will dictate which of the many possibilities for applying psychology and related knowledge are chosen. It is reasonable to assume that social workers, counsellors, teachers and community workers, even doctors (not to mention those the professionals are accustomed to calling 'lay people'), also apply psychology to a greater or lesser extent. However, while we would expect many people to have a working knowledge of psychology, as psychologists might be expected to have a working knowledge of sociology, anthropology, etc., it would be right to turn to a sociologist or anthropologist for more extensive knowledge of that particular field, and it is also right for a psychologist to be asked for specialist psychological knowledge. The least that should be said of a psychologist is that, if he does not have the appropriate psychological knowledge immediately to hand, he knows where to look.

Modified participant observation is currently being utilised by Sheffield psychologists in connection with several projects in the community. These include a 'truancy centre', a project concerned with the education of gypsy children, and support components to a mothers' action group and a community rights and advice centre. This is described as 'modified' participant observation because the psychologists are in fact occupying a more specific role than was the case in the early Norwich and Huddersfield work, although a far less formal role than is usual in other contexts.

As community development and community education expand and come closer together, we are more likely to see the comprehensive campus incorporating facilities for mothers' groups, counselling centres, play groups and toy libraries. The community toy library is a particularly good setting for the communication of information on factors affecting child development and thus *giving away* psychological knowledge rather than affirming psychological expertise. The parallel in school-based work is the in-service education programme for teachers. The emphasis should be on facilitating the work of teachers in ways which enhance the potential of schools for meeting children's needs in a fully humane and personal way through the curriculum and through the organisational patterning of relationships. Sheffield's emphasis in this area is on the curriculum of 'health and personal relationships' and on the structure and sensitivity of 'pastoral care' resources. These are areas in which the psychological service clearly has objectives in common with the education welfare service, youth workers, doctors, careers officers and social workers, as well as with teachers and educational advisers; all of whom are concerned directly or indirectly with the pupils and their families and collectively with the education and welfare of the community.

A Sheffield project which has been very much a product of cooperation between the psychological service and the education welfare service has investigated the relationship between prolonged absenteeism amongst school pupils and factors such as poverty, the size of schools and suspension rates (Galloway, 1976b). By including social, organisational and attitudinal factors, this research provides a context within which the psychologists and other workers concerned are able to evaluate their own work and some aspects of educational policy. Research projects, by and large, are more public and accountable activities than casework, and therefore have greater potential for mobilising opinion and resources in the direction of constructive social change. However, there will always be client-centred work, for schools will never be perfect communities which meet the total diversity of human needs, and adaptation will always be a two-way process.

A greater emphasis on the broader needs of the community should be a natural development for educational psychologists if they keep in step with the progress of education itself. The education service is already thinking in terms of life-long education and thus of meeting the recurring needs of the whole community. Community centres, youth · centres, the work place and the home are all locations where education is constantly taking place. There are many needs to be met in addition to those of the child in school. Adults frequently wish to learn new skills, both basic and advanced, which directly enhance the quality of their lives and by extension the lives of their families. This aspect of education is of growing importance. Adults who are 'returners to learning' in a formal sense, often wish to improve their actual study skills. Many are interested in the subject matter of human development itself and in the psychology of human relationships, social and ecological psychology. A goal of the community-oriented psychologist should be to facilitate the acquisition of the subject matter of psychology and to interpret its relevance wherever possible. Community psychology should be seen as more a style of operations than a professional speciality.

We should not forget the educational needs of the aged. While it is taken for granted that the young need to learn to meet the demands and responsibilities of adulthood it is all too easy to forget that preparation for life's stages is incomplete unless we also prepare for the later stages of ageing. There is a persistent myth that people always deteriorate intellectually with age. In fact, research in psycho-gerontology has shown that this is not inevitably the case (Riegel and Riegel, 1972; Schaie, 1974). It seems rather, as though a social process takes place which treats the old as though they are incapable of learning. 'Ageism' is as discriminatory as racism or sexism. Not many changes could be more in our general interest than the reversal of this process: we must all anticipate the possibility of becoming old! The apparent intellectual deterioration of many very old people is frequently aggravated by withdrawal from intellectually stimulating activity, and often exacerbated by inadequately compensated sensory defects. The old people's home and the geriatric ward are perhaps the least protested social scandals of our 'civilised' society, in that they are frequently places where confusion and deterioration are unwittingly promoted. If we negligently sought to exterminate the personality, dignity and finally the will to live of a human being, admission to a geriatric hospital almost seems designed for the purpose (Robb, 1967).

This may seem a long way from the concerns of educational psychologists, but this may be because those concerns have been far too parochial. Of course I am not advocating that today's educational psychologists should start adding psycho-gerontology to their already too extensive list of activities, but possibly a community psychological service of the future would take this speciality under its generic wing. I am sure there are clinical psychologists who would be quite happy to leave the health service. Educational psychologists should be preparing for a merger.

In conclusion I would like to offer the suggestion that since psychology is a root discipline of education its contribution should be radical. To achieve this, not only do we need a psychology of learning processes, but also a discipline which comprehends the psycho-sociology of the developing person in the changing community and addresses itself to social change. As Iscoe (1974) points out: 'A community psychology that makes its living dealing only with the casualties of the social system will soon lose its viability. It should be proactive rather than reactive, adhering to a fundamental tenet of public health that no condition is ever prevented by treating the victims of the condition itself.'

By all means let us continue to assess the skills of handicapped infants as long as no one else can do it better, but let us not believe that the psychology of handicap, of toys and play, of families with handicapped members, of community needs and social policies, ends here.

8 SCHOOLS' SYSTEMS ANALYSIS: A PROJECT-CENTRED APPROACH

Robert Burden

Educational psychology training courses do not exist in a vacuum. To operate successfully within a community with an existing school psychological service they must needs take into account both the practices and ideologies that already exist within those services. Any course tutor seeking to impose his own radical ideas upon an existing psychological service within which he had no official status would almost certainly doom his course to failure. This is, in fact, not an altogether unhelpful state of affairs since, without revolution, change is inevitably a slow process that is best brought about by negotiation. Any training course failing to take into account the attitudes and reactions of those receiving its trainees would only be doing a disservice to the latter. To borrow an apposite phrase from Georgiades and Phillimore (1975), there is first a need to 'cultivate the host culture'.

In Exeter the emphasis on the changing role of the educational psychologist has evolved gradually since the inception of the educational psychology training course in 1972. The fact that it has been able to do so has been due in no small measure to the co-operation of the Local Education Authority and its schools and to the receptivity of its School Psychological Service. The main impetus has come from a recognition within the University School of Education that such institutions ought not to exist in splendid isolation but should be actively involved in offering their resources to the community. In the present instance this has involved members of the educational psychology training course working in close co-operation with members of the local authority system on joint projects of mutual benefit.

The beginnings were small and could hardly be described as radical by any stretch of the imagination. In 1973 the Exeter Education Authority, still at that time independent from Devon, asked the School of Education for help in setting up an in-service training course on approaches to remedial reading. The contract that was established was that this would be undertaken on condition that any such course could be incorporated into some aspects of the training of educational psychologists. (This important notion of *contract* is one to which I shall return later.)

What developed was a joint enterprise, the details of which have been described elsewhere (Burden, 1974) in which the trainee educational psychologists carried out a series of attainment and diagnostic tests in the participatory schools on children whom those schools considered to be failing in reading. Where this began to differ from the traditional approach was that the trainees acted as consultants in showing the teachers how to administer the tests for themselves and how to interpret the results in a meaningful fashion; and the subsequent lectures and seminars on approaches to remedial reading were directly related to the expressed needs of the teachers during the preliminary assessment sessions. Moreover, responsibility for the organisation and presentation of these lectures and seminars was undertaken jointly by the course tutor, the trainee educational psychologists and the teachers themselves.

The main point that needs to be emphasised here is that this was the first major step in the evolution of a style of working that has subsequently undergone a number of significant developments. The university training course was offering the services of its trainees as consultants, not as students, to teachers in local schools with a general problem that the latter wanted solved. The trainees did not go in with ready-made solutions; they went in with a particular initial approach strategy (i.e. diagnostic testing) that they offered to 'give away' to the teachers. They also offered information on possible problem-solving strategies (i.e. lectures and seminars on remedial reading) that was directly related to the expressed needs of the consumers. Finally they committed themselves to working *with* the teachers rather than *for* them in helping the latter to furnish their own solutions to these problems.

A completely different project the following year led to another important milestone in the development of the consultancy model. This came to be known as the *Dart* project and arose directly from the concern of one of the local educational psychologists about the system of pastoral care that existed within a newly formed comprehensive school. A large number of children had been referred to the School Psychological Service by the school counsellor but little effective change had occurred in the handling of 'problem' children within the school despite the educational psychologist's expressed opinion that in most cases the problem did not lie within the children themselves. It was felt that a team of trainees working within the school on one day per week throughout a term might help to clarify the situation and effectively alter the teachers' attitudes towards educational psychology.

Although the school counsellor had been fully involved in the setting up of the project, it became clear at the start, from a note she had circulated to other members of staff, that her perception of the educational psychologists' role was very much one of 'testers'. In fact, a list of thirty-one pupils for testing had been drawn up prior to the trainee group's first visit to the school! However, a strategy meeting by the group decided that it would be counterproductive merely to try to see as many children as possible, and that instead each trainee should concentrate on working with two pupils throughout the term with a view to analysing those pupils' problems within their total social context.

There is an important point to be made here. It is sometimes felt by educational psychologists who wish to move from the more traditional role to that of school-based consultant that this automatically entails the immediate abandonment of individual work with children. In the Dart project we learned that to attempt such a sudden switch will almost certainly prove disastrous. Teachers have certain expectations of educational psychologists, usually centering on the individual assessment of children. They will not readily change those expectations just because they are told to do so by educational psychologists. What the psychologist must do is to use the results of his investigation of the individual case *to widen the teachers' appreciation of the context within which problem behaviour is occurring.*

It was only by starting with descriptions of their involvement with individual children who had been referred to them that the trainees working on the Dart project were able to persuade a full staff meeting to discuss the important issues underlying the referral of such children for 'help' in the first place. The kind of questions that could then be presented to the staff took the following form:

1. What is the school's attitude to problems? What constitutes a problem for them? In what terms do they construe their problems? i.e. what is the meaning of the term 'problem pupil' for that school *as a whole*? Is there a school ethos? What does the school think should be done about problems? Whose responsibility is it to take action?

2. What is the school's attitude towards educational psychologists and other similar outside agencies? What are the school's expectations of the educational psychologist? Do these match those of the psychologist? Can any disagreements re expectations be satisfactorily resolved? (Such questions are equally valid for any individual member of the school staff as for the school as a whole.)

3. What is the exact nature of the problem referred? Who says
that it is a problem? Does anyone disagree? Whose problem is it: the
child's, the teacher's, or the school's — or all three?

4. Can any problem ever be seen in isolation? Is information
necessary about all aspects of the total situation in which the child is
functioning?

As a result of such discussion it proved possible to reach agreement
with the majority of the staff on a number of future lines of action.
Perhaps the most important of these was that the school and its
individual teachers should attempt to become more aware of their own
biases and ways of looking at things; that they should also be aware of
their expectations of helping agencies and whether those expectations
matched those of the agencies themselves. Lines of communication had
been opened and wider possibilities made available for future intervention by educational psychologists. The process by which this had been
achieved was far more threatening to all concerned than ever occurs within the traditional model, but further steps had been taken towards the ideal
of true communication between professionals by means of negotiation.

The following year's *Priory* project has been described in detail elsewhere (Burden, 1976). It has particular significance within the present
context because it enabled us to recognise for the first time the way in
which the school-based projects had not only become an important
aspect of the Exeter training course but also were reflecting a crystallis-
ation of our ideas about the changing nature of the educational psychologist's role. Here the request came directly from the school concerned,
a comprehensive with some 700 pupils and a newly appointed head of
remedial studies. The contract on this occasion was that the course
tutor together with five trainees should again work at the school one day
per week throughout a term to help in the establishment of appropriate
remedial provision.

It subsequently became clear that it is at this very point that the
successful outcome of such a way of working hangs in the balance.
Despite the fact that the Head of the Remedial Department not only
had an excellent working relationship with the course tutor but was
also a straightforward person who was not afraid to speak her mind, it
was not until half way through the term that we discovered a complete
mismatch of expectations. The headmaster, both remedial teachers,
various other members of staff and the educational psychologists themselves all had very different ideas about the kind of role that they ex-

pected the latter to play, despite apparently complete agreement at the start of the project.

This experience led subsequently to the formulation of two principles, basic to success in projects of this nature. First, it is important not only to establish a contract between the parties involved, but also to ensure that such a contract is made explicit *even to the extent of writing it down*. In this way it can be examined and agreed upon by all concerned and referred back to on any subsequent occasion where conflicting expectations seem to be arising. Secondly, it is equally important to convene regular feedback meetings to which all members of staff in any way involved with the project should be invited. If one member of the team, e.g. teamleader, only communicates with one high status consumer, e.g. head-teacher, the possible number of misunderstandings will be increased enormously. Similarly, the notion of shared responsibility can only become reality in an atmosphere of mutual trust which in itself can only be engendered by two-way communication within the group context. It may well be that the resentment expressed against many organisation and method studies stems from this very point, that such studies are imposed from without and rarely occur within the context of a mutual problem-sharing exercise, the successful outcome of which is recognised as depending upon the allocation of shared responsibility.

A further principle that emerged with some clarity in the Priory project mirrored an aspect of the Dart project but also marked a significant development from it. This centred upon the importance of finding the right kinds of questions to ask *at the start* of any such project. At Priory it was decided that little progress could be made before certain vital questions were considered. These took the nature of: (a) What is meant by 'remedial' within the context of this school? (b) How can we best identify remedial children on admission to the school? (c) What further specific diagnosis is needed for each child? (d) What are the most effective treatment and teaching methods to use with these children? (e) Who needs to know the information gained from (c) and (d)? (f) For how long and in what form should remedial assistance be continued? (g) What are the criteria for remedial success?

The production of this list of questions and its presentation at a meeting of all concerned led to the setting of clearly defined objectives for the educational psychologists' involvement. We were now all employed on a joint enterprise with specific goals that were either within reach or could be seen as in need of redefinition or restructuring. Some of these goals were reached fairly painlessly, but as far as others were concerned, only limited progress could be made in what seemed to be a positive direction. The important point here however, is that we were building in a means of evaluating the effectiveness of our contribution as educational psychologists to some of the problems with which this comprehensive school was faced. We were no longer able to fall into the common trap of assuming that we could provide 'one-off' solutions to problems, nor could we take it for granted that whatever course of action we decided to take was *ipso facto* appropriate. For their part, the school staff were forced to specify exactly what they hoped to derive from their interactions with the educational psychologists and to justify their reasons for their expectations.

What was emerging by now was not only that we had been involved in several worthwhile projects providing actively different learning experiences for the trainees but also that such projects could be linked together by an as yet ill-defined underlying rationale. But where was the theoretical structure within which such a rationale might be made more explicit? There seemed very few leads within the then known structures of educational or clinical psychology (although it later transpired that a search through the literature of industrial psychology would have proved far more helpful, viz. Georgiades and Phillimore, 1975; Miller, 1976).

The answer, when it came, followed on directly from a day conference on systems theory held at the Royal Society in London and attended on impulse by the author. This led to an immediate recognition of the potential value of systems theory to the kind of projects with which we had become involved and a search of the literature in this field. An excellent starting point was an Open University set book of readings on *Systems Behaviour* (Beishon and Peters, 1972) in which an article by Jenkins gives a clear and concise introduction to the systems approach.

Jenkins points out that the systems approach to problems is a way of replacing a piecemeal approach by one that attempts to look at problems *in their overall context*. He begins by outlining the properties of systems as complex groupings of humans that can be broken down into interacting sub-systems usually forming some kind of hierarchy. In order to function at all any system must have an objective, but this in itself will be influenced by the wider system of which it forms a part. Usually, systems have multiple objectives which may well be in conflict with one another, thereby making it necessary to have an overall objective which effects a compromise.

Systems engineering involves four distinct stages: (a) systems analysis,

(b) systems design, (c) implementation, (d) operation. It is mainly the area of *systems analysis* that is of primary relevance to us here, and this in itself can be broken down into a number of clearly defined stages. In order to highlight the relevance of this approach to school-based projects, I shall illustrate each of these stages by reference to some aspects of the projects described above.

Stage 1. Recognition and Formulation of the Problem

The questions to be asked here should take the form of: How did the problem arise? Who are the people who believe it to be a problem? Is it the right problem anyway? Might it not be just a manifestation of a deeper or different problem?

In the case of the Dart project, it only became clear by chance that by no means all the staff saw the problem in the same way or even recognised that a problem existed. By asking the first question we were able to establish that the amalgamation of secondary modern school pupils into an existing grammar school to form a comprehensive, whilst seeking covertly to maintain the ethos and much of the curriculum of the grammar school, was having a disastrous effect on the attitudes and responses to school of a significant proportion of the pupils. Moreover, by looking beyond the manifest behaviour of this group of apparently 'maladjusted' pupils, we were able to discover that the lack of clearly defined rules of pastoral responsibility or structure within the school was making it impossible for even those with the children's best interests at heart to be sure of what was appropriate with regard to their level and method of involvement.

Stage 2. Organisation of the Project

It is important here to arrange as wide as possible terms of reference and access to any necessary information or person. The project must be properly scheduled to ensure that its completion is feasible within the allocated time and a critical path analysis worked out in order to concentrate maximum effort in the most important areas. Teamwork is essential and each person in the team should have a specific role and/or function to perform, e.g. leader and co-ordinator, systems engineers taking an overall view of what is going on, designers, statistics expert, economist/accountant, plus at least one consumer.

This is an area that had not been given clear enough consideration up to this point, although it had been recognised on a number of occasions that some of the anxieties and frustrations felt by some group members had been due to uncertainties about role and function. On the other hand, it could be argued that to organise a project with this degree of specificity has certain inherent drawbacks. There is a danger that imposing too structured a framework for investigation early in the life of the project could create artificial barriers to the production of important information that might be more readily forthcoming in less formal situations. The distinction here seems to be between deciding fairly quickly upon the most relevant information to be gathered and setting about gaining this in as efficient a way as possible, as opposed to a much more reflective and reactive way of working that requires an initially more passive style of response. Certainly, the latter way of working seems to be implied by the method described by Rabinowitz (1977) and his observation that a period of gradual involvement within a school taking anything up to two years is a reasonable timescale on which to work. It seems probable that the amount of time available is an all important variable here with structure becoming increasingly necessary as the timescale diminishes.

Stage 3. Definition of the System

The next task is to define in precise terms the system which is to be studied. This is a process of analysis whereby the system is broken down into sub-systems, which in turn should lead on to the task of synthesising these sub-systems so that they work together towards achieving an overall objective. Thus, in the Dart project, it was an analysis of the inefficient functioning of the pastoral sub-system that led to a deeper understanding of the school's manifest problem, while at Priory it was important to view the organisation of the remedial department with regard to its place in the hierarchy of sub-systems, i.e. other departments within the school.

Stage 4. Definition of the Wider System Which Contains the System Being Studied

It is important to consider the environment in which the system is operating. This is usually very hazy at first, so a good deal of clear thinking is needed to construct the conventional flow-block diagram. This has not played a large part in the projects described here, although it would have been impossible to make sense of the situation at Dart without a wider consideration of the issue of compulsory comprehensive education and its effect on the attitudes of the school staff and the local population. An excellent illustration of the more sociological aspects of this particular issue in relation to school studies is provided by Hutton (1976).

Stage 5. Definition of the Objectives of the Wider System

There are likely to be several objectives, often conflicting and usually forming some kind of hierarchy, and unless these are clearly defined they will not be able to contribute effectively to the major aims of the wider system but will tend instead to pull in different directions.

When examining the function of a junior system such as a remedial department, it may be more productive to face up to the aims and objectives of senior systems such as English, Maths and Science departments than to ignore them. As in the case of Priory, the meaning of 'remedial' within the context of a school can most profitably be considered in the light of basic criteria set by other departments in order for pupils to achieve the objectives that those departments have set. Thus the remedial sub-system can be seen to contribute effectively to the wider goals agreed upon by more senior sub-systems within the school.

Stage 6. Definition of the Objectives Within the System Under Study

However great the resistance to the formulation of objectives and the establishment of quantifiable criteria, this stage is essential in order to monitor the efficiency of the system. Once the systems engineer has clarified these objectives to his own satisfaction, he must gain the agreement of all concerned and make sure that everyone is conversant with any decisions reached. This was a lesson ignored at Dart but learned under pressure rather late in the day at Priory. It certainly helped a great deal in the final positive response to the Priory team's recommendations as compared with the hostility voiced by some staff members to the issues raised in the final staff meeting at Dart.

Stage 7. Definition of the Overall (Economic) Criterion

The more precise the objectives the easier it is to set up quantitative criteria. Even if the latter are only qualitative, they should be simple and direct, and related to agreed objectives. In practice, confusion can often arise because of the application of contradictory criteria. At Priory for example, one remedial teacher's criterion for success was a happy, unpressurised group of children, and she therefore placed little emphasis on educational attainment, whereas her senior colleague was working towards the goal of reintegrating the pupils into the mainstream of the school and saw the only way of achieving this as being through the improvement of attainments in the basic subjects, even if it meant forcing the children to work harder than they had ever before. This was a central issue not recognised as such before our intervention but merely seen by certain senior staff members as a source of minor irritation.

Stage 8. Information and Data Collection

This is the most extensive stage of the investigation. As many key people as possible should be interviewed and all sources of information explored. The data obtained will be required not only to provide information about the current operation of the system but also to make forecasts of the environment in which the system will have to operate in future. There are many ways in which educational psychologists can obtain such data within the school setting, ranging from informal interviews to structured questionnaires of the kind developed by Findlayson *et al.* (1971) to the application of repertory grid techniques in the manner described by Leach and Raybould (1976). We have found the analysis of classroom interactions according to behavioural principles to be particularly helpful especially when the educational psychologist applies such an approach in following through a pupil's day, i.e. accompanying the same class or pupil from lesson to lesson throughout the day and assessing the different interactions between that pupil or class and various teachers.

Jenkins points out that much of the work involved in this kind of approach will require the active participation of many more people than the systems team. However, there are certain key roles that a systems engineer should play. (a) He has to sort out what is going on – to distinguish the wood from the trees; (b) he stimulates discussion and obtains agreement on objectives, (c) communicates agreed objectives, and (d) takes an overall view of the project to ensure that techniques are used sensibly. (e) Within this overall approach he brings together various specialisations, (f) decides when any activity should stop, (g) bears in mind cost-effectiveness, (h) constantly challenges assumptions, and (i) sees that the project is planned to a schedule, priorities are decided, tasks allocated and that the project is finished on time. Next, (j) he explains clearly and concisely what the systems project has achieved and presents a well-argued and well-documented case for implementation, at the same time ensuring (k) that the users of the operational system are properly briefed. Finally, (l) he makes a thorough retrospective analysis of system performance.

The parallels that can be drawn between many of the insights that we were able to reach as a result of the relatively unstructured team projects described above, and the kind of results that have been claimed within management theory for systems analysis (Immegart and Pilecki, 1973) led to an intensive search of the systems literature. The purpose here was to seek a design within the field of systems analysis that might serve as a suitable evaluative framework for future school based projects. A very promising model was found in the CIPP analysis (CONTEXT, INPUT, PROCESS, PRODUCT) described by Stufflebeam (1968).

Stufflebeam starts with the premise that evaluation is the science of providing information for decision-making, i.e. that rational decisions can best be made on the basis of information obtained through formal means such as setting criteria, measurement and statistics. Where he differs from the usual psychometric approach, however, is in suggesting that in the ongoing context of an educational programme this information can best be gathered *not* by means of the limited hypothetico-deductive method and the even more limited experimental-control group design, but by careful consideration of the Context, Input, Process and Product of the programme.

The major objective of *context* evaluation, which should be carried out at the programme planning stage, is to define (a) the environment where change is to occur, (b) that environment's unmet needs, (c) the problems underlying those needs, and (d) the opportunities for change (see p. 126). At the end of this stage the information gathered should lead to the establishment of goals and objectives.

Input evaluation should provide information on how to utilise resources to meet these goals and objectives best (see pp. 127-8). Its aim is to identify and assess the capabilities of the system, the human and material resources, with appropriate strategies for meeting the programme goals and possible designs for implementing those strategies. At the end of this stage it should be possible to analyse the potential costs and benefits involved in alternative procedural designs. The overall purpose is to work out feasible programmes for introducing change.

Process evaluation follows the approval and implementation of the plan of action. Its purpose is to provide periodic feedback of information to those involved in the project that might lead to refinements in plans and procedures. The objective here is to detect any defects and monitor the potential sources of failure (see pp. 128-9).

Product evaluation is concerned with relating outcomes to objectives, as well as to context, input and process information. It is here that the effectiveness of the project is determined by defining criteria for the successful attainment of objectives and measuring whether these have been reached. Decisions can then be made as to whether to continue, terminate, modify or refocus a change activity (see pp. 129-30).

The opportunity to test out this evaluative model was provided by the request from a primary school set in an educational priority area for the educational psychology course to become involved in helping to improve the standards of reading of the pupils in the school. This became known as the *Larches* project.

In setting up, organising and attempting to evaluate the Larches project a conscious attempt was made to incorporate the lessons learned from previous projects within a systems theory framework. First, the project was set up at the specific request of a high status member within the school acting on behalf of the staff who were generally concerned about the high proportion of children moving on to secondary education with very poor reading attainments. Secondly, the involvement of the trainee educational psychologists was discussed at a full staff meeting at which the psychologists were present. At this meeting a number of points of agreement were reached which were written down by the psychologists' team leader and re-presented at the following week's staff meeting in order to establish that they were a true record of the contract agreed upon by all parties. Regular weekly meetings were arranged, at which everyone involved agreed to be present. Careful notes were kept on everything that occurred and these were discussed independently by the project team and submitted by one of its members to a CIPP analysis. Finally a 'termination of project' meeting was arranged at which the project team presented the staff with a written record of what they felt had been accomplished during the time of their involvement and where they felt the most profitable future lines of action for the school staff might lie.

On 23 September 1976, the University team attended their first staff meeting at Larches. The main purpose of this meeting was to establish some form of generally acceptable framework within which the project could take place to the mutual benefit of all concerned. The following major points emerged:

1. The University team should attend the school every Tuesday, apart from half term, during the period 5 October-23 November (seven sessions). They should arrive at 10.00 a.m., work within the classroom until 4.00 p.m. and then be available for staff discussions from 4.00 to 5.00 p.m.

2. Since it later transpired that each of the ten class teachers in the school was willing to have an educational psychologist working in his or her classroom, it was arranged that each psychologist should spend the morning session in a Junior classroom and the afternoon

session in an Infants or Nursery classroom.

3. The psychologists would have lunch at the school in order to allow time for discussion with the teacher with whom they had been working in the morning.

4. A general staff meeting should be held every Tuesday in order to review the work carried out during the day, to exchange general impressions, ideas, frustrations, etc. and to plan the following week's programme.

5. It was agreed that each psychologist should work out with the teacher with whom he or she was working, how best use could be made of their joint skills.

6. However, the work carried out in the individual classrooms should always be related in some readily identifiable way to the main purpose of the exercise, i.e. the improvement of reading standards within the school *as a whole.*

It was considered important that realistic expectations were set by both sides. The University team agreed that the school had a right to expect (a) objective professional expertise that could be utilised in assessing some of the problems faced by the school in different kinds of ways; (b) informed opinions on different available methods of improving children's reading standards; (c) realistic advice on how this might be achieved in individual classrooms and the school as a whole; (d) the introduction of various materials that might be appropriate to these aims; (e) the introduction of various tests and techniques designed to diagnose specific problems; (f) honest and professional feedback on how well individual teachers and the school as a whole were achieving their agreed aims; (g) a high level of commitment to working with Larches teachers as a *team* engaged on a joint exploration of an area that should be of future benefit to the majority of the children attending the school.

It was not considered realistic to expect that the reading ages of a large number of children should suddenly shoot up overnight or that instant solutions should be provided to deep-rooted problems – only that sensible suggestions should be made as to how the school might begin on the long-term task of achieving a permanent increase in overall reading standards.

As far as the school staff were concerned, it was considered realistic for the psychologists to expect (a) the freedom to work in whatever professional capacity seemed appropriate within the school; (b) a commitment to the enterprise that transcended personal anxieties or defences regarding outside intervention; (c) an openness to giving fair and honest consideration to ideas from others, however fanciful these might sometimes appear to be at first; (d) open feedback at every stage on their reactions to the progress being made; (e) a commitment to accepting the educational psychologists as colleagues in a teamwork approach to the reading problems within the school rather than as magicians or whipping boys.

It was not considered realistic that the school should make any sudden changes on the basis of the psychologists' recommendations alone — but rather that a majority of all concerned should feel a clearer sense of purpose and direction with regard to the improvement of reading standards within the school, together with a rational belief that steps were being taken to accomplish this.

Extracts from CIPP Analysis of Larches Project

Context

(a) A description of the school with regard to pupil numbers, structure, aesthetic properties, staff numbers, names, and responsibilities, and the environment in which it is set.

(b) The major unmet need of the school in this context was to develop a coherent, structured approach to reading throughout the school such that both staff and pupils could recognise an integrated progression towards certain specifically defined goals.

(c) Some of the problems underlying those needs were the needs of individual teachers to develop self-confidence and gain the respect of their colleagues; the poor and unstimulating home backgrounds of most of the pupils and the rather bleak nature of the school buildings. Teaching methods were unsystematic and varied greatly throughout the school; record keeping was sparse and incompetent. There was no carefully planned progression from one class to another. Teacher assessment of reading was confined to a few individual teachers and even in those instances not relevant to the problem. Staff morale was generally poor due at least in part to the high degree of informal control wielded by one high status member who strongly advocated formal teaching methods. This teacher's views were influential although held only by the minority.

(d) On the positive side, the staff on the whole clearly recognised that there was a problem and were concerned to do something to solve it. They were interested in the children's welfare and did their best to provide a caring environment. This was reflected in the children's positive attitude towards their teachers and the school.

Input

(a) The school had a number of largely unrecognised human resources. Two of the staff had pursued advanced courses in remedial reading and the part-time remedial teacher had twelve years' experience and many ideas which had not been used to their fullest advantage. The majority of infant and lower junior classes enjoyed reading and showed great enthusiasm for books. However, this enthusiasm seemed to fade at the top end of the school. There was also a fairly wide range of reading materials, SRA kits, and equipment such as record players and tape recorders. These resources were not being used effectively partly because several of the teachers with knowledge and ideas tended to be self-effacing and hesitated to suggest changes and improvements. Some good ideas and helpful suggestions had obviously been ignored in the past because of the power structure within the school and the staffroom hierarchy of control. One of the important goals of the project was the need to bring about a restructuring of this hierarchy in order to establish an atmosphere conducive to the free expression of constructive ideas by equal partners.

(b) The input brought to the situation by the educational psychologists was first, that of experience and knowledge of materials, tests and reading techniques. The teachers were shown how to use diagnostic reading tests and began to systematise their reading records as a result of individual and group discussions. One input session involving a visiting speaker centred upon the notion of infant screening and the early identification of reading problems; another was held at a local independent school specialising in behaviour modification techniques; while yet another introduced some videotaped presentations of children from various classes talking, working and playing.

(c) A variety of strategies were used in attempting to meet the project goals. Each psychologist worked individually with two class teachers and used whatever strategies seemed appropriate. Some teachers felt defensive and vulnerable which meant that the psychologist concerned had to be tactful and reassuring. In some instances the psychologists had to display their own teaching competence in attempting to model good teaching and management techniques. A great deal of additional information was fed back to the staff on individual children with whom the psychologists had specifically been asked to work.

(d) The overall procedural design utilised techniques from a variety of psychological and sociological methods. Selective praise and behavioural management techniques were used, as also were counselling, modelling and the giving of information and advice on request. While most of these techniques were familiar and well-tried in other contexts, their use in this particular combination formed a design relatively new to the practice of educational psychology. As such the design could be said to be experimental and open to continual modification as the project progressed.

Process

The regular end of the day group/staff meetings provided an important planning and decision-making function as well as providing feedback to everyone. As a feeling of mutual trust began to grow, so it became possible to bring out individual teachers' strengths and discuss ways in which these could best be utilised within the school as a whole. A number of different but related lines of action stemmed from these discussions. The teachers with a great deal of knowledge about reading who had previously offered little to other members of staff, gradually began to accept responsibility for introducing such ideas as informal reading inventories, the need to cross reference by level of difficulty of reading books from different schemes, and ways to develop reading comprehension in conjunction with recognition skills. Sub-groupings and factions within the staff began to emerge more clearly at this point, but it was to their credit that a suggestion from the psychologists to split some of the staff meetings into smaller work-study groups was resisted in the interests of staff unity. It was decided instead that staff should work in pairs during the week to produce information and possible lines of action on what the whole group agreed to be the four main areas in need of improvement throughout the school.

Not all the feedback was positive. Individual anxieties began to emerge from both the staff and the psychologists. The experienced remedial teacher clearly felt threatened by our presence and tended to be overlooked by the team; the high status authority figure felt under attack and made various overt attempts to sabotage constructive efforts by other staff members; and the person with responsibility for initiating the project began to display his own anxieties about the outcome. The members of the project team all displayed feelings of confusion and expressed their concern that a satisfactory outcome might not be reached. It was here that the written contract proved so valuable because it provided a reference point to which people could turn in times of stress.

It became clear in retrospect that this was an area on which more of

our attention should have been focused. Personal conflicts were eased
over by diplomacy, some anxieties were alleviated by creating an
atmosphere of constructive optimism and joint commitment, and the
structure of power within the staffroom hierarchy was subtly altered in
favour of the more skilful and knowledgeable members. However, it
could be argued that these were in many respects superficial and transitory effects that were unlikely to last beyond the period of intervention. It may be at this point, therefore, that the application of techniques from the realms of social psychology, possibly even taking the
form of sensitivity group training, could helpfully be introduced. Again
it can be seen that the demands placed upon an educational psychologist working in this way require a different kind of professional expertise than that required within a more traditional model — and this in
turn has implications for those involved in the training process.

Product

The immediate outcome of the Larches project appeared to be an optimistic, enthusiastic and grateful staff. Changes had occurred in the
physical appearance and organisation of some of the classrooms and in
the methods used by some of the teachers. Since these were closely
associated with many of the suggestions made by team members during
interpersonal and group discussions and were allied with positive verbal
comments from the teachers and gestures of friendship from the pupils,
the project could be accounted successful on that score alone.

More importantly, however, by the end of the term the staff were
well on their way to producing a developmental reading checklist which
was to be implemented throughout the school. This checklist was to
cover the four main areas that the staff felt to be most important in the
children's reading development: (a) a basic sight vocabulary, (b) the
child's level of phonic skills, (c) the most appropriate level of various
reading schemes, i.e. readability level, and (d) language comprehension.
When completed, this checklist would provide a framework within
which every child's reading progress could be recorded on a hierarchy of
objectives, and which every teacher could use.

Informal follow-up some three months later produced the information that the checklist was in operation and that regular staff meetings
to discuss its most effective implementation were continuing to be held.
The staff themselves also produced two information pamphlets on the
work they were doing. Group testing of reading attainment at the top
of the school had shown a marked improvement in overall standards but
the timescale involved makes it unlikely that this success could be attri-

buted entirely to the intervention project. It seems more likely that the dedication and determination of some of the staff had been beginning to show dividends and that our intervention had been able to build on this.

Further efforts had also been made to establish much closer contact with the children's homes and to establish a parent-teacher association. However, there were likely future problems in that one of the project's most active supporters left to have a baby, the LEA decided to withdraw the services of the part-time remedial teacher, and the project initiator was actively seeking promotion to the headship of another school. This illustrates the weakness of even the best short-term intervention projects in that a great deal of consolidation and long-term support is needed in order to ensure that initial enthusiasms are maintained and subsequent pressures resisted.

Three final points need to be made in concluding this description of what has undoubtedly been our most successful project to date. First, a written summary of the psychology team's conclusions on what had been achieved during the intervention period was produced for the staff for discussion at the final project meeting. In this way it was possible to reach a consensus of agreement on which of the agreed goals had been reached and to discuss why others had not. We were able to avoid any tailing-off effect and to end the project on a positive note. Secondly, partly for the purpose of the training exercise but also to stimulate improvement in the model, the individual team members were asked to produce their own accounts of what had happened during the project and their evaluation of its success. The general feeling seems to be summed up in the words of one trainee who described the project as 'very useful, difficult, controversial and time-consuming . . . from a personal point of view fascinating, involving, tiring, confusing, fun and at times a headache'.

Lastly, it could be argued from a strict systems viewpoint that the project had been a failure. We had neither specified precisely our objectives nor established our acceptable criteria for success. This point has been touched upon earlier with reference to the work of Rabinowitz and highlights our current dilemma. Should the next step be to tighten up on this aspect of the intervention process? Or should it be to accept that there are some situations where the early setting of objectives could prove counterproductive and to seek ways of identifying the factors within a situation that make one or the other approach more likely to be successful? It is the resolution of this issue that we intend to explore in our next project.

In this chapter I have tried to describe the way in which a particular interventionist model that can be successfully applied by practising educational psychologists has developed out of a dissatisfaction with the more limited 'individual-child-crisis-type-referral-system', or 'motor-mechanic' role that educational psychologists have been both trained for and expected to play in the past. Nothing that has been described here could not have been implemented by an educational psychologist working together with a small team involving, say, a remedial advisory teacher and social worker; or even, if needs be, working alone and consciously performing the key roles of a systems engineer as described by Jenkins. This is not to denigrate the part that educational psychologists can play in helping to find solutions to problems faced by individual children, parents and teachers. The argument rather is that only by viewing such problems within the wider context of the institutions and environments in which they occur can the psychologist be in the best position to discover where the real problem lies, and help to provide *from within these environments* themselves the kinds of strategies that are likely to be most effective in achieving satisfactory solutions for *all* concerned.

In order to achieve this aim it has been necessary to develop a totally different methodology from that which has previously been considered appropriate. This in turn has necessitated the exploration not only of other fields within psychology itself, e.g. social and industrial, but also those disciplines such as sociology and systems theory that have hitherto been ignored or treated with scant respect by practising educational psychologists.

9 YOUR SERVICE: WHOSE ADVANTAGE?

Frank Carter

You are a Head-teacher; Miss X comes to you expressing concern about Michael: he's a nuisance, he's way behind in his reading, he's never on time for school, forgotten his PE kit again, punched little Nigel again, swore at the dinner-lady . . . You have had enough of Michael: makes no difference what you say, what you do, the boy is uncontrollable, gets no guidance from home, the same with his older brother . . . No use contacting his parents, all they say is 'hit him', 'don't stand for it, we don't't'; they are both out all day, most evenings too . . . call in the Psychologist.

You are a Paediatrician: Simon you have known since the antenatal days; mother in particular had great difficulties in accepting that her baby was unlike the others in the maternity wing; hers was described as 'a mongol'. You explain Down's syndrome, you instruct and coax mum and dad into trusting that something can be done for Simon. You advise on management, but approaching school-age, Simon continues to present major problems of coping, of retarded language, and of concentration. You refer to the Psychologist.

The 'individual case' referral. You as Head-teacher might ask in Michael's case, what do you not already know, what areas are you not free to investigate yourself, what have you tried to do, what have you not tried, what do you expect a psychologist to do that you might not do yourself? What novel lines of approach might the school pursue? And how many more Michaels are there? Perhaps there's something about that class? this school? this area? the lack of meaningful parent-teacher contact? Perhaps that teacher's approach is altogether too inflexible? the curriculum is inappropriate? Perhaps Michael and the others you would refer to the psychologist are somehow symptomatic of a management problem in this school. The possibilities seem endless, the probabilities however are few. The probabilities were known too to the Paediatrician. When you met Simon at age two, you could anticipate

The seeds of much of the above paper were sown in the course of discussions and in a subsequent report written in conjunction with my friends and ex-colleagues, Pat Bragg, Pat Cleaver, Tracy Cooke and Ken Leeming. My gratitude to them.

that at four years he would be presenting the difficulties which you in turn presented to the psychologist. The parents wanted clear guidelines to stimulate their son's development then. They needed the reassurance and support of other parents then.

Michael? that was in February. Now it's the end of May. Michael had to wait his turn on the psychologist's waiting list. By this time the situation you recognise as rather altered: possibly school is more tolerant; the boy seems less aggressive, more amenable, and his work is improving. Things always pick up in the summer term; besides, he'll be in the deputy-head's class in September. The Ed. Psych. arrives, observes Michael in class, takes him out alone for an hour or so. You have to fill in for an absent member of staff. When you emerge the Ed. Psych. is gone. But he is diligent. In two weeks you receive his report: Michael is of average ability but his reading age is twenty-three months behind his chronological age, the home background is unstable, the child is attention-seeking and immature; he needs intensive remedial teaching in the security of a small group. A number of considered judgements here; how much Psychology? This contribution will have cost the psychologist three or four hours of his much sought-after time. In effect he has tidied up the information you had already, given it a form, and made you a recommendation you feel you cannot implement.

Simon's Psychologist has a particular interest in 'the assessment of the pre-school handicapped' and everyone knows he has, so he is inundated with referrals. Simon is of statutory school age in eight months time; no point in 'seeing' him before then since no place will be available in Special Education until some time later. You continue to ward off his anxious, beseeching parents, knowing how busy the psychologist is with his individual cases. Finally you hear from him: Simon has Down's syndrome, his parents are anxious, his IQ is 55, his attention-span short, concentration limited; Simon should start at the nearest ESN(S) school the following month. The educational psychologist refers to the child as a suitable candidate for a programme of behaviour-modification. You wonder if Simon's teachers will comprehend the terms, the jargon in which the advice is couched, and be able to implement the recommendation. You doubt if the parents will understand it. Not sure if you understand it yourself . . .

The individual case. One of many on a waiting list. Assess the child. Use your intuition and standardised norm-referenced tests. No one tests like a Psych. tests. And what are the advantages? For Michael and

Simon, their families, their teachers, the referring agents? Is this the
most effective use of an educational psychologist's time, competence,
training, energies, influence – to whittle down a waiting list,
preoccupied exclusively with individual casework? Assessing the child,
as distinct from assessing the skills and the needs the child has at this
point in his development – all at someone else's behest as distinct from
being prompted by some form of preliminary psycho-educational enquiry. Advice to parents, teachers and others on the basis of the same.
What gains is Psychology making? What is Education gaining? How
many children actually gain? In the main what the psychologist has
done is to use a standardised norm-referenced test enabling comparison
between the individual performance and that of the norming-group,
often in accordance with a construct of dubious worth and meaning.
No provision here for a breakdown of the individual's skills, what he
actually can do; or for effective teaching based on behavioural objectives; or for educating parents as the prime agents of change; or for a
teaching/learning model more appropriate and more useful than the
clinical, paramedical one; or for ensuring that Psychology is reaching
out across greater numbers and into the spheres of greatest influence.

You are a Psychologist: your concern in the process of education
prompted you towards qualification as a LEA Ed. Psych. Now after a
hundred or so Michaels and Simons you begin to wonder if all your
effort on their behalf is in any meaningful sense productive. What you
have learned to do best is to administer and to interpret tests; now you
ask of what relevance to Michael or Simon is your hard won IQ? Can
this information help the child's teacher? his parents? You think you
have gained some hitherto elusive insight into what to do now to pro-
mote the child's education, but you are far from sure that your advice
will be heeded, that your recommendations will be implemented. Your
work is so organised that your real influence ends when the child
leaves your presence and you have reported your findings. Certainly
you are able to remind yourself of your undoubted individual successes,
but now pause to reflect further whether the psychology you have
disciplined yourself in might not have uses in the broader spectrum of
the learning process. You might start looking at the learning of one class
of schoolchildren. You find you have something to offer many of them
. . . you help to structure the material of the curriculum to take account
of developmental needs, to break down reading into its component
skills and devise means of positioning a few 'non-readers' on a skills'
hierarchy such that the teacher can immediately tell what to teach next;

you apply principles of operant-conditioning to help some children gain control over their own behaviour . . .

Then the bell tolls: the waiting list summons. Your errant attention is demanded. Do not respond. Reject that call. You have nominal responsibility for ten thousand children of school age. Possibly one fifth of them will be referred to you. Not counting those of pre-school age, that's a lot of individual assessments . . . and you personally will have selected very few indeed of that number as in want of your attention. You pause again to reflect: what scope is there for innovation of thought and action in a profession whose clientele is initially selected by people of other professions? By people whose professional training, if any, is often vastly different from yours? So you ask yourself: of what relevance is my training for the job I now do? Do I want to devote my intellect, sensitivity and energies to the daily task of putting out other people's fires? At the risk of straining the analogy it is worth considering that fire brigades may have a certain superiority over most psychological services since they not only put out fires but also try to prevent fires spreading, and to prevent fires starting. They teach other people how to douse the flames, how to avoid creating situations which risk conflagration.

The historical antecedents of practitioner psychology have been largely in the realm of the abnormal, the difficulties and aberrations of learning, the problems of adjustment. Comparatively little is yet known about how marriages remain stable, how people cope successfully with adversity, how children learn to read, what makes for successful teaching; faith, intuition, conscience are phenomena. If a training in psychology does nothing else it does highlight our extraordinary ignorance about human behaviour in all its varied manifestations. When bringing psychology to bear on education the Educational Psychologist is offering fewer untested assumptions, a less passionate, a more objective viewpoint on the problems of educating young people. Psychologists are given a training in behavioural science. Because the various graduate and postgraduate courses emphasise different aspects of this, and because experience as an Educational Psychologist slants different psychologists in different directions, the profession of Educational Psychology is a heterogeneous one. Most Educational Psychologists have had some time in classroom teaching and most will have specialised interests and abilities. The background indicates the need to adopt a generic role, while the personal limitations and persuasions argue in favour of developing a specialised contribution for application across the board, to exert an influence in the field of mainstream education.

In terms of the skills peculiar to the educational psychologist it must be obvious that he has more to offer an LEA than psychometric assessment of the individual child. In an education authority of say, 200,000 children, with hundreds of teachers, advisers, administrators and others, there are usually at most twenty professionals who are trained in the behavioural sciences. Psychologists themselves must make clear how their training can be put to best use.

Consider: you are an Ed. Psych. employed in an LEA. You have been taught to approach educational matters involving cognitive, social and emotional development in a relatively objective fashion. You enquire into any educational 'problem' according to your own lights. You have to formulate the problem, you question, hypothesise, collate all available information. You analyse and interpret in terms of a theoretical framework, you make use of whatever methods you have at your disposal, including statistical techniques, in pursuit of practical solutions to educational problems. You test your own and other people's assumptions. In practical terms, you are quite probably testing the progress being made in some area of development of children. If the need is to compare a child or children against the attainment level of the peer group, then you employ tests which have been reliably and validly standardised and are norm-referenced. But since the greater need will be to enquire into the relative strengths and weaknesses of the individual, and of many individuals, then you use criterion-referenced measures which specify to the person responsible for teaching, where to teach. What are you testing for, you must first clarify.

You can help formulate objectives, expressed as performances, that is: in behavioural terms. You specify the behavioural outcome anticipated by the instruction given, the conditions and the criteria of acceptable performance. If the child succeeds in achieving the required outcome, the teacher can move him on to the next stage in the teaching/learning strategy. If the child does not succeed, you can at least question whether the instruction given was adequate, sufficient or appropriate. Thus there is evaluation of the teaching and the method. These days of concern with 'standards', what other professional is developing any kind of objective yardstick whereby to compare the good, the bad and the ugly in education? Besides which, and not entirely by way of accidental spin-off, this type of approach affords the practising psychologist opportunities to assess his own competence, measure his effectiveness, evaluate his own level of performance, as stringently as he would the performance of children, or indirectly their parents and teachers.

Educational psychologists are often keen to dispense with psycho-metry whilst advocating that teachers working *in situ.*, directly with their captive clientele, should be provided with in-service training given by psychologists in how to administer quite similar tests. Devolution of the testing burden must take place, but if the profession could turn its attention to the twin issues of what to test for and what to test with, educational psychology could be offering an invaluable tool. There has been the very rapid development in the last decade in the UK of work with the multiple and severely handicapped, in the use of observational techniques by educational psychologists in conjunction with the children's teachers and parents. Like the technique of writing objectives, such practices deserve to proliferate further in special education, but also beyond and into the classrooms of all schools. As a behavioural scientist, the psychologist has skills to offer at all points in the education process, and positively to seek opportunities and situations to devolve his skills to those who can use them.

The basic and perhaps unique role of the psychologist in an LEA is now being depicted as 'questioner'; the issues may be presented for formulation into a questioning format that lends itself to testing for solutions. The efficacy of any proposed solution is also being subjected to scrutiny. Educational evaluation becomes integral to the educational psychologist('s) functioning. The educational psychologist can aim to exert an influence over and to evaluate mainstream education, instead of forever preserving the doubtful *status quo* by giving children labels which channel them into 'special' facilities that have known advantages for the administrator though not necessarily for the child's education. Furthermore, as questioner, the educational psychologist is parallel in function to the educational adviser. You are also an adviser, not in the sense of advising in a specialist scholastic field such as French, Maths, etc., but you do advise likewise from the position of specialist training and experience — in Psychology. You develop a co-working partnership with educational advisers, as with teachers and parents. Advisers have the pulse of the district schools and generate innovations in education. Membership of or participation in advisory teams is a prerequisite to the psychologist's making any impact in the scholastic areas wherein his most useful work can be done.

How you are now going to operate, and the levels at which you will operate effectively require attention. The first priority must be to find alternatives to a debilitating referral system. The assumption is that a system dependent on the referral of individual children by all agencies,

educational, administrative, medical, social, is non-viable where LEAs
employ small numbers of psychologists, although they all have something to contribute in the broad field of mainstream education. There
are at least two strategies which can be adopted: the use of screening
techniques; and getting to know your schools.

Screening tends to be used to investigate those children in any given
community who may have special educational needs. As with other
forms of testing, you need to know what you are doing the exercise for.
In the long term you will be providing the Authority with information
on which it may plan for future resources. But the shorter-term gain will
be if your screen can provide information about areas of skill deficiency
such that immediate programmes for remediation can be put into
effect. Again the advantage lies with the screening instrument that is
criterion-referenced as opposed to some kind of normative measure.
Thus an investigation into the reading standards of a given age group in
a number of schools is of limited value indeed if all it yields are 'reading
ages'; but of great practical advantage if it affords the schools as well as
the investigator a breakdown of the phonic skills achieved by every
child screened. Your job as educational psychologist for the area, in
compiling the suitable items, organising the assessment procedure, is
certainly a tricky one. As with any planned investigation on such a scale
you co-operate with colleagues quite likely to have greater expertise
than yourself, in this case the peripatetic remedial staff and educational
advisers. Apart from the primary purpose of helping children to learn to
read, you will also be influencing teaching methods and curriculum
content, as well as utilising and possibly contributing to the psychology
of learning and child development. To screen in order to provide information enabling children to learn and teachers to teach more successfully in the short term surely justifies the exercise. Screening for 'at-risk'
factors, except in a parochial context such as investigating the background of a comprehensive's first-year intake, seems to offer no such
short-term advantages. The move towards infant screens which aim to
identify whether 'learning preconditions' have been established in the
pre-school years can offer no immediate gains either, unless teachers are
prepared to train four- and five-year-olds in the skills of attending,
listening, co-operating, fine manipulation, etc. The principle is: screen
for information that can be used. Meanwhile, there is an obvious need
for research into screening; where better to research it than in our
schools?

Getting to know your schools when your LEA is still groping
towards implementation of Summerfield proposals, seems a decidedly

silly proposition. However, you can get to know the schools of greatest need first, another function served by your screening device. Moreover it is soon apparent that some situations do not welcome psychologists, feeling they cannot use their services. But make an impact in a neighbourhood establishment and your utility will be publicised. Advisers are a fount of information about their district schools; tap this source. For as you familiarise yourself with various educational establishments, you are growing aware of the dynamics of the social situations in which or on which you must work. Informal contacts are established − often your most efficacious line of referral, since here is where anxieties may quickly be alleviated and preventive steps taken. Your 'way in' to the bigger schools is probably through the remedial departments: teachers responsible for the 'slow learners' and the 'maladjusted' are lonely souls in the large comprehensives; they will respond to your invitation to meet their counterparts in the locality. Then you have a forum in which teaching methods and resources may be shared; you gain hitherto unavailable insights into their thinking and organisation, and you forge links at vital points in these vast school communities which can shape a daunting commitment into a manageable perspective. The model of the parent-teacher workshop is still little utilised; one of its many advantages is the in-service training facility it offers the educational psychologist to appreciate the perceptions held by the school's staff and, most enlightening, the parents, about their children's development, adult attitudes and coping strategies, the ethos of the local community, and so on. Again the need to research is paramount: into communications systems, the social psychology of the group, employment of the paraprofessional in training parents in techniques of training their own children: the educational psychologist has ample opportunity.

Now you çan envisage operating at different levels: at the level of the individual, of the group, of the district and of the whole authority.

The psychological service being offered does concern itself with individual children. Individual children will still reveal themselves from the screening process and through the educational psychologist's everyday contact with the whole range of educational facilities his area provides. And what is to stop other agencies channelling into the educational system at least some of their expertise and sufficient, useful information to which the educational psychologist can refer if his intervention is required? But you must resist the temptation to pose as some kind of consultant, as middle-man between the schools and all the extraneous helping professions; then you are anybody's. Let yourself be seen to get your intervention in where your feet are − in the educative process. Direct personal intercession by the psychologist is justified when all the indications are that only this would enable effective remediation to ensue. Your principal aim would be to identify the individual whose needs can best be met, initially anyway, by your personal involvement. Your personal philosophy and approach would determine the framework in which you set your objectives: whether you provide 'therapy' or 'treatment', 'remediation', 'teaching', or 'modification'; whether you 'back hunches' or 'test hypotheses', apply an 'interaction model' or whatever. The theoretical model espoused is probably founded on convenience or conviction; in any event you are faced with the task of aiding someone to learn — scholastically, socially, emotionally, developmentally. And this is a vain pursuit unless the milieu in which this person has known failure is taken into account.

Consequently, you operate at the level of the group: which tends to mean, the school. By now you know something of the children, and the staff of the school in question. You are familiar with the regime, its methods, its aims, its atmosphere. You have information concerning the circumstances around the 'problem', within the establishment and the home. You contract with teachers and/or parents to co-operate for the child's benefit. On the wider front you can collaborate with pastoral-care staff, advisers, the administration and related agencies. School-based projects are part and parcel of your week's programme; devolving assessment, observation, evaluation and modification skills into the classroom; involving in curriculum innovations and educational surveys and research, which directly affect the school or schools in your patch. The individual is a social animal; your sphere of involvement comprises the nursery, the playgroup, the home, the hostel, any community. You may be keen to de-institutionalise your role, recognising that education does not stop at sixteen: your field includes the 'higher learning' establishments, as well as the local hospital and old people's home. In all you are to assess the influence of the group on the individual and use that influence; how is the individual adjusting to the norms of the group? how is the group coping with the expectations of the wider community? how is the group reacting to the behaviour of the teacher? You sit in on the work of the class, say; agree with the teacher criteria for identifying children's responses as 'on-task' and 'off-task'; record the frequency of each type of behaviour; record the teacher responses to each behaviour; the teacher may learn she is reinforcing the inappropropriate behaviour. A design in need of some refinement! — but intended to sketch the hypothesis-testing exercise affording instant feedback, not to some referring or consultative agency, not to some jealously guarded file, but to the critical situation itself, the stage of human interaction.

The district perspective of the educational psychologist's job implies not only an educational bias but a community involvement and awareness even more so. Symbiosis: as you gain knowledge of the area schools, you learn more about the district served by them. The more you know your district, the clearer your understanding of the ethos of the schools. In your educational/scholastic hat you work the round of schools, learning to accept and be accepted by different heads and staffs, advisers and local officers. You are forever emphasising your preventive commitment, your willingness to devolve techniques and skills into those situations where they can be of most immediate use, and stressing your concern to evaluate the educative process. You survey the needs of the area with a view to contributing towards plans for any future eductional resources. Suppose there is an outcry about disruptive behaviour in the local comprehensives. You ask each headteacher to collate all relevant data in the experience of each school; formulate a number of hypotheses about causes of disruptiveness in schools; test and feedback information to all sources. Solutions should be forthcoming either in terms of some kind of new provision, or in organisational changes within each school. Contact with pupils' families is axiomatic in ventures aimed at major modifications in attitude and response patterns; you begin to piece together a picture of alienated youth reacting to the frustrations of low school achievements, peer-group pressures to conform to a morality at odds with parental priorities, and various schismatic influences within the family structure. What are the pressures, the values, the influences peculiar to this area? The political, religious and industrial tone and character assume significance. The educational psychologist must be sensitive to their significance. On this point, liaison with the range of helping agencies and organisations becomes essential. Join a team of social workers for a few days. Set up a multidisciplinary discussion forum to examine the admissions, reviews and discharges of children in special education locally. Home visits: your comfortable ideas are shaken when you see and feel what living on the isolated farm is like, what it means to have dad at sea or down a pit. Schools reflect and are reflected in their communities, their social environments, with far-reaching implications for all concerned.

Clearly descriptions of different levels of operation indicate the changing emphasis the educational psychologist places on the different aspects of the job. As an LEA psychologist you may be one of a score who individually and collectively may be able to exert some constructive influence on the educational climate and direction taken by your

County, City or Metropolitan Borough. At this level, a psychological
service cannot afford to become associated exclusively with the Special
Schools Department, making it responsible in function to the Assistant
Director, Special Education. A viable and effective service contributes
to education and to the LEA not to one of its departments. The depth
and range of services provided at the individual, group and district levels
should be reinforcing this point daily. The LEA's psychological service
should be providing survey data, describing and formulating the
problem areas, the areas in need of development. It should be investigating for solutions, presenting information and recommendations to
the Authority's planners and policy-makers. An LEA is as likely to be
moved by political considerations whether to build a nursery or to
channel funds away from, say special education and into open-plan
developments in infants schools. Since, or even despite the fact that
psychological services are in the main innovations on the education
scene, your LEA is as likely to pay more attention to the deliberations
of administrators, advisers and head-teachers advocating that a 'need'
exists for a school for children with communication disorders, a residential facility for the 'maladjusted', or whatever. A psychological service can make useful inroads here. The educational psychologist can arm
himself with factually based data and being accountable to the population he serves, can make known his recommendations to the Director of
Education, to the Education Committee, to the governing bodies of
schools, to members of local government and Parliament.

Psychologists who are Education Department-based are, by definition of their role and function, inescapably community-based. Indeed
when an LEA looks beyond its responsibilities to stock and staff its
institutions, it can begin to explore avenues which open up opportunities for all sections of the community to discover new skills and adapt
old ones, to learn and to continue learning as a life-long pursuit. Now,
this could mean costly expansion on the Further Education front; but
it could mean a concerted effort to divorce education from the need to
establish educational institutions, or at any rate, alternative institutions
might be sought other than schools and their like, which carry the
implication that all that is worth learning has to be learned therein.
Alternative learning institutions could be in the form of learning
systems and resources available to all. Again, the need to research
tutoring models, the instructional utility of the media, the creation of
new industries, crafts, art forms. Shaping the education offered and
nudging it in what directions — these tend to be the expectations of
advisory staffs, which would include the psychologist. His main contri-

bution in turn would be in posing the appropriate questions and striving for solutions about the learning process, in whatever field and at whatever stage of development. Once you interpret your role in this way, you must be alive to educational change and to the expectation that your skills can be applicable in the entire educational service.

Ultimately, you are forced to decide that you cannot be master of all trades; if you are offering a service of any value, its limits will be defined even though its potential be great. You uphold your generic commitment but develop specialist interests and expertise. Freed of a system and load of individual referrals, your 'specialism' will not be interpreted by your educational psychology colleagues as an invitation to shunt all 'specialist cases' in your direction. The specialism does however become the focal point in the overall service for all known information, including research and practice, in a given area. The specialist makes up-to-date information available to colleagues in the employing authority, co-ordinates the practice and resources within the psychological service, liaises with academic sources . . . there is no shortage of activity feasible and germane to various aspects of professional psychological development. Furthermore, proven professional competence rather than administrative flair is the basis in an egalitarian service upon which career opportunities may be provided. Otherwise psychological services, like most other professional services, will follow the crass, wasteful practice of promoting to positions of seniority the most accomplished practitioners, bestowing administrative responsibilities and paper work while depriving the trained professional of client-contact. On the other hand, no matter what the criteria it uses to push its people into senior positions, a hierarchical psychological service can ensure its voice is heard where it matters; it will affect no system and service of education if it is not and is not seen to be an integral part. A generic educational psychologist who has a specialist contribution fits the framework. You have more to offer your colleagues and your employers. You are developing assessment and evaluation techniques across the board and particularly within your own specialism. You are devolving the increasing skills gained from your discipline in practical and academic psychology, on to the shop-floor. You are exerting a constructive influence on mainstream education. You are providing a vibrant and viable service.

10 THE PSYCHOLOGIST'S PROFESSIONALISM AND THE RIGHT TO PSYCHOLOGY

Andrew Sutton

The future wealth and prosperity of our country depends not upon the finite and limited stores of fossil fuel lying beneath our continental shelf, but upon the minds of our children. Vast energies are being devoted to exhausting our oil and gas over the course of the next generation, but hardly any account at all to how that generation itself is to be developed. And when those physical resources have run out we shall have to live upon our children's wits, just as by now we should have been living on our own, had not the lucky chance of North Sea oil bailed us out for a few more years.

How we educate and bring up our children is therefore everybody's business not just that of their parents and their teachers. The recent 'Great Debate' shows the dawnings of political awareness of this problem, but the level at which this debate has been conducted indicates that the complexities of the processes involved are as yet but dimly perceived by many of those responsible for crucial decision-making. Concern over standards and steps to assess and monitor them are not in themselves enough to understand the means whereby standards are achieved; demands that children should fulfil their potential will result in only limited returns if we are not to question how 'potential' itself is to be enhanced. Yet the quality of official attempts to review and compare practice (e.g. DES, 1977) is scandalously inadequate, and unless major changes and improvements are brought about in the level of technical expertise of everyone concerned then this huge and vital sector of our economy may very likely let us down over the years that we will need it most.

Childhood is a phenomenon unique in nature, during which the specifically human traits of abstraction and conscious thought are developed in the growing child in the course of his interaction with adults. The dependence of human personality and intelligence upon the transmission of culture from one generation to the next has permitted the vast extension of human achievement over the course of historical development, and offers us the opportunity to manage and direct how our children grow up, *as long as we know how* (Vygotskii, 1956, 1960; Sutton, in preparation). Ineffective practices, in this field as in any

144

other, will fail to gain their hoped-for results, however much we may wish them to.

The goals that we set as a society for bringing up and educating our children are of course political, moral and economic questions, of direct personal concern to every citizen whether he has children or not. So to a degree are the means by which these goals are to be attained. But the actual day-to-day methods adopted by parents, teachers and everybody else whose activities impinge on the world of children, are also technical matters. If we as a society decide that we are not concerned with the intelligence and achievement of the next generation, their personality and behaviour, then we may happily leave the formation of these traits to the spontaneous effects of whatever might occur. But if we wish to have a say in how these things turn out, then we must recognise that we are dealing with the most complex phenomenon in nature, and that the techniques that we adopt will have to be worked out and refined with far greater care and rigour than we have devoted to such relatively simple projects as supersonic flight or nuclear power. Pedagogy, whether the informal activities of parents and community or the formalised activities of the school system, *must* be a science if we wish to exercise any control over this aspect of our lives.

There are many disciplines that might make a far greater contribution to our educational practices than they have made to date. But the core problem in the whole educational process is the means whereby skills, knowledge, attitudes, values and so on, are actually transmitted and internalised. If we do not understand this then the whole system is based on guesswork and we will muddle on from hunch to hunch without evaluation, remaining the victims of spontaneous natural forces to a degree now unthinkable in so many other everyday fields. Education and child-rearing, if they are not to remain *ad hoc* enterprises out of keeping with the rest of our technological society, need to be rooted in a sound base of developmental psychology, which itself must be directly relevant to the day-to-day problems of bringing up and teaching children.

It cannot be emphasised too strongly that the necessary knowledge is *not* already available amongst the many professionals and experts who are involved with our children in a wide variety of contexts. Certainly there are a host of individuals whose life experiences and other factors have contributed to intuitive skills and approaches, but without rigorous scientific examination and evaluation these skills will always remain personal gifts, unavailable to the far greater numbers who do not possess them. Certainly too, there is now a plethora of 'professions' who profess competence in their fields by virtue of their professional training. For example, teachers know how to teach, social workers how to 'treat' delinquents, psychiatrists how to 'cure' problems of living. But in reality it is a dangerous professional who does not learn very early on in his career just how little of relevance or of use has been imparted to him by his professional training. And of course we already have a psychology (several in fact), but there can be few who work with children who have not been disappointed in what it can contribute to their work. Yet to recognise the limited contribution of psychology to date is not to deny the urgent necessity of a practical developmental psychology for the future, a psychology closely linked to the realities and needs of our society.

Which brings us to educational psychologists.

There are now about 800 educational psychologists working in local education authorities in England and Wales, and more than a hundred new entrants a year coming off training courses. The work of educational psychologists brings them routinely into direct personal contact with individual children and their families, it involves them with teachers, head-teachers and educational administrators, with their local social services departments, the National Health Service and a wide variety of other agencies, voluntary and statutory, concerned with growing children. This large body of psychologists would seem ideally placed to make a significant contribution to our understanding of how children develop in our society and of the effectiveness of our present systems for fostering their development. They could relate theory to practice, evaluate present provisions, and help to generate and test new theory based on what is found to be effective.

Burt, 'the first educational psychologist', had envisaged his work as largely scientific research in which the study of individual children would play an important part (Burt, 1964), and the investigations that he undertook on this basis in the years following the First World War were widely influential in shaping provisions made for failing and delinquent children. But subsequent educational psychologists found themselves enmeshed in the 'child guidance' and 'mental health' movements (Keir, 1952; Wall, 1955) and educational psychology became in effect another helping profession, like social work and psychiatry, with scientific research playing little or no part in most educational psychologists' work (DES, 1968). The numbers of educational psychologists have doubled over the last decade, and their training qualification has been upgraded to a masterate, but there appears to have been no widespread change in the extent to which their professional work involves scien-

tific research. Professional developments over this period, as in other
local government professions, have tended to be structural or bureau-
cratic in nature rather than scientific or technical.

The major changes that have come about in English education over
the time that educational psychologists have been establishing themselves as a profession have not stemmed from a scientific on-the-spot
analysis of the practical problems of the education service, conducted
by local education authority psychologists. They have come from elsewhere. These changes, the swing to more informal teaching methods,
discipline and school organisation, increase in the size of schools, a
lessened stress on the 3Rs, 'pastoral care' and so on, have not occurred
suddenly, but by a process of encroachment, from school to school,
authority to authority, offering unparalleled opportunities for the careful comparative evaluation of changes in practice before universal
adoption. Local education authority psychologists have been in a
unique position to monitor and evaluate the effects of these changes.
They have not done so. Similarly over this time there have been a
sequence of 'crises' within the education system that have been the
subject of widespread and often uninformed public debate. These have
included the blacks, school illiteracy, non-attendance, teachers'
problems in controlling their pupils, all issues in which educational
psychologists are closely involved in their day-to-day practice. Yet
educational psychologists have made no significant contribution towards
the public understanding of how these crises arise or how they might
most effectively be met, and the public debates have been conducted
without benefit of scientific fieldwork and analysis. These issues themselves remain unresolved.

It would be all too easy to suggest that the reason for the educational psychologists' failure to contribute to these important questions
lies in the poor calibre of the psychologists in local authority employment, or the irrelevance of psychology generally, or both. But it will be
argued here that the determining factor has been the particular organisational structure under which educational psychologists work, a professionalisation linked to the status of local government officers rather
than of scientists, or even of help-agents.

Change in local government practice (up until recently usually
related to expansion) has usually occurred independently of scientific
investigation. A noticeable principle that has appeared to underlie much
of the expansion in provision is the process of 'more of the same'. The
law of 'more of the same' appears to operate thus: if x number of staff
exercising a certain skill cannot make inroads into a given problem,
then $2x$ doing the same thing surely will. This approach is usually

advocated most strongly by the particular professional group most directly involved in the given problem, and psychologists have as a profession been subject to the same law. Where psychologists have not been involved, however, is in the examination of the particular actions and activities that are failing to produce the desired results, or the validation of the prediction that what is required to meet a given need is more staff, better paid, doing the same things as before. To make such an examination might be to offer more psychology, but would not necessarily require more psychologists. It would also bring the educational psychologist into potential conflict both with other people's personal and professional ambitions and with the very structure of local authorities, their schools and their agencies. Most practising educational psychologists are surely aware that the overwhelming majority of individual problems that they deal with are essentially ones where proper scientific investigation cannot in honesty be restricted to the 'problem child', the 'problem family', etc. but must also involve the agencies of society that have defined the problem and which may themselves provide the sole situation in which it is manifest. Yet these agencies are often those of the local authority itself, leading to an inexorable pressure upon the psychologist to compromise his investigations.

Educational psychologists have earned the stereotype of 'testers', but testers of children rather than of hypotheses. They remain closely associated with a variety of practices and provisions the effectiveness of which is open to serious question. The individual intelligence test remains an important routine procedure even in problems such as poor reading or delinquency where its results are rarely relevant to understanding the problem defined. Child guidance lacks demonstrated value (Shepherd *et al.*, 1971); remedial teaching does not necessarily remediate (Miller, 1976); observation and assessment centres provide little relevant information to justify their cost (Cooper, 1975); children are placed together in ESN(M) schools with no necessarily common educational needs (Sutton, 1977a). It may be significant in view of educational psychologists' historical involvement with child psychiatry that such practices often relate to a pathological rather than a psychological model of children's problems and needs. But it remains scientifically unjustifiable that such massive psychological resources should be invested in servicing and expanding these provisions while their basic effectiveness remains to be demonstrated. It is worth noting that the first cautious steps of clinical psychologists out of the psychiatric hospitals and into the community (specifically, health centres) are subject to continuous demands that their effects be validated (Stuart,

1977). Yet educational psychologists continue to ask for more (Association of Educational Psychologists, 1975) as if there could be no possible question about the benefits offered, and greater establishment is sought to provide (rather than evaluate) further 'services'. Screening for educational problems, early intervention, prevention, etc. may be very worthy social provisions, but are they useful, or are they possibly counterproductive? We do not know, and judging from past performance we shall still not know even after their widespread introduction. Effecting change in teachers' practices by laying on in-service training courses might have immediate face-validity (at least to non-psychologists), but the psychological fallacies involved in this approach are well known elsewhere (Georgiades, 1975) and would soon re-emerge in their familiar forms, if only they were put to the test.

To catalogue such professional inadequacies in the practice of educational psychology, it must be affirmed again, is not to suggest that its protagonists are all either fools or charlatans, nor does it deny the benefits that psychology could offer the educational system. The structures and processes of an organisation are the major links between human and technical inputs on the one hand and the output of the organisation on the other. The particular professionalism of educational psychologists is therefore an essential key to understanding the educational psychology that they provide.

Educational psychologists have entered their profession by various routes. But the present glut of graduates from training courses probably means that for the immediate future the majority of entrants will have passed through one-year postgraduate courses. Prior to this professional training most of them will have worked as teachers at some time or other, yet though the necessity for this teaching experience is often hotly debated this is another matter which has never attracted scientific study. On becoming educational psychologists the new entrant, nowadays often in his mid-twenties, earns a fairly substantial salary. Annual increments thereafter are proportionately small, but after only two years he may be promoted to a 'senior' post, and at any time he is eligible to be a 'chief' or 'principal', in charge of the psychological service of a local authority. At no time after completion of basic professional training is the educational psychologist required to undertake further professional training, and no higher professional competence needs to be demonstrated as a condition for promotion. In some places the custom has sprung up of 'senior' psychologists supervising the work of non-senior colleagues. In most cases the senior posts indicate an administrative responsibility (usually for a geographical area within a local authority), though in others they represent a specialised field of work, such as co-operation with social services departments, and increased specialisation is sometimes advocated as a future focus of professional development. Appointments and promotions for 'chief' or 'principal' posts might involve elected representatives as well as administrative staff, whilst posts at other levels are more likely appointed by the psychologist in charge of the service along with other administrators. The general pattern of the professional structure is similar to that of many of the other professions with which the educational psychologist will find himself in day-to-day contact.

However satisfactory, or otherwise, such a structure might be for the other professions that share it, particular problems arise for psychologists because of their status as scientists and the increasingly pressing need for scientific involvement with our system for bringing up and educating children. Perhaps the high entry salary indicates some recognition of this scientific status, perhaps it is no more than a historical accident, but whatever its reason it provides an attractive career prospect for graduate psychologists.

One may sometimes hear the claim that educational psychologists' training takes seven years (three years honours degree + one year postgraduate teaching certificate + at least two years teaching + one year masterate), though in effect the first degree may include hardly any human psychology and it is hard to see how the teacher training and teaching experience could prepare for work as a *psychologist*. The seven years might represent a series of happenstance experiences rather than a co-ordinated, sequential training, with only the content of the final year comprising a planned and deliberate preparation for the career ahead. But once through this year professional preparation and development are over. Educational psychologists, unlike clinical psychologists, rarely have time guaranteed them to undertake research or incentive to further their own studies once they are in post. The educational psychologist may have a potential career-life of forty years.

After two years educational psychologists may, if they so wish, apply to become associates of the British Psychological Society (and qualify therefore to bear the letters ABPsS after their names). Admittance to the associateship is virtually automatic to graduates from British training courses who have served the required two years, and are willing to pay the requisite fee. There is no need, either for this recognition or for promotion within local education authority service, to undertake scientific work. Indeed the general model presented to those moving into the profession is that administrative 'safeness' and the production of conventional versions of psychology-as-she-is-spoke are more likely to be associated with professional advancement than are some of the things that they might have hoped to do when they were on their training courses. The phenomenon whereby newly qualified professionals abandon what they have been taught in favour of the culture of their employing organisation is well-known to occupational psychologists (Georgiades, op.cit.), though the dynamics of the situation, the reinforcers and constraints which determine this change in behaviour, should be more closely studied by psychologists when they occur within their own ranks.

With no requirement for additional professional accomplishment or expertise above the entry level as a prerequisite for promotion, and with the balance of rewards weighted towards non-scientific endeavour, educational psychologists' easy slide into their present irrelevant position has been inevitable. Their professionalism depends upon outside forces, primarily within their employing institutions, to determine the type and quality of work that will meet with preferment above entry level, and thus 'educational psychology' as a profession must be regarded as a career primarily within the local government service, rather than within psychology. The contradictions inherent in this position cause tensions which will probably increase in the foreseeable future. There is the problem of the relationship between 'senior' staff or 'chiefs' and their non-senior minions. The higher grade staff may have risen to their present positions after long years in the job, or they may have been drawn up rapidly into their present posts after only brief practical experience during the period of rapid professional expansion in the early seventies. Either way, they need possess no particular psychological skills or virtues to justify their higher salaries and supervisory status. But the present cutback in professional expansion cuts off the lower grades from prospects of similar posts in anything but the distant future. These factors, prolonged over a few years, can lead only to discontent. Tensions might be further exacerbated by the increasing tendency of new entrants to regard themselves as 'psychologists', as distinct from our older generation who tended to see themselves as 'educationalists' and the psychologists in charge of services who are drawn inevitably into the role of 'administrators'. And whereas at one time it was fairly easy for discontented psychologists to leave the profession to free themselves of its frustrations (see DES, 1968), the present economic situation has trapped such dissidents firmly within the system, even cutting down on lateral mobility between local authorities. The new larger local authorities with their swollen psychological services contain potential splits between staff that may overtax management structures designed and appointed for the easy implicit consensus only possible in a time of professional confidence and expansion.

The nature of relationships within the profession is not the only ethical concern for psychologists, nor even the most important. The most immediate moral dilemma that faces educational psychologists relates to the question 'who is the client?'. Any professional (or any citizen for that matter) may be placed in a situation where he has to decide between public and private good, but the educational psychologist's position as 'a servant of the authority' brings in a third factor, his supposed loyalty to his employers, that may be expected to override both personal and public responsibilities. He cannot offer the direct, professionally responsible relationship enjoyed by a doctor and his patient, even though his relationship with children and their families might be outwardly conducted as if this carefully defined and safeguarded situation actually existed between them. As long as no conflicts of loyalty occur, then relationships do remain honest and secure, but as soon as the interests of the employing authority are involved then there arises the very real risk that the clients' rights of advocacy (Sutton, 1977b; 1977c) are very much at risk. Moreover, the educational psychologist has no direct access to the community at large. His terms of service, for example, make it unthinkable that he should campaign publicly against inadequacies that he knows mar the school system in which he works: rather they demand that his contact with the community, other than at the individual 'clinical' level, should be mediated by his employing authority. Many educational psychologists feel that their duties and responsibilities ought to lie first and foremost towards their clients, towards society, and towards their own integrity as scientists, and only secondly towards their employing institutions. It seems likely that most parents consulting an educational psychologist would assume that he would be able to think, and act, according to such a system of values. It appears equally likely that most educational psychologists' employers would take it very amiss if their psychologists indeed thought, *and acted*, according to the above priorities.

For the educational psychologist is employed to serve the local authority, not the community in which he lives or the scientific discipline for which he has been trained. To work in any other way would be to make the activities of the authority potentially visible, and therefore accountable, and to cause conflict with other groups within the authority. The real application of psychology means seeking alternative ways of doing things, not seeking even more psychologists to support present systems. The decrease in school population and the present economic strictures have hopefully curtailed the immediate excesses of 'more of the same', but a wider lesson may have to be learnt. Increasing the number of psychologists may very likely identify an increased number of problems *ad infinitum,* but without a return to serious psychological investigation there is unlikely to be any increase in the solutions identified for these problems. Educational psychology has professionalised itself into the position of a bureaucratised help-profession. The technical and organisation problem is therefore how to ensure that at least some psychologists are able to relate directly to the needs of individuals and of society as a whole, so that the bulk of our developmental psychology manpower is not directed into the service of necessarily conservative institutions. If the above analysis is correct, then we must now direct our concern towards devising alternative structures and processes in which developmental psychologists might work.

Perhaps a thousand psychologists in England and Wales work with problems of bringing up and educating children. Some of these are clinical psychologists in the National Health Services, some teach at colleges and universities, some work in research establishments. But the majority, the overwhelming majority when it comes to the potential for working directly with normal children in their normal life situations, are the 800 educational psychologists. As suggested above this virtual monopoly presents a monoculture too uniformly susceptible to the constraints of its own professional structure. We need instead social and policy initiatives to respond to a wider range of demands and produce a wider range of contributions to our national needs.

Many alternative professionalisms might be suggested for psychologists in this field, and tested out in practice. Outlined briefly here is a suggestion for a profession of developmental psychologists who would work directly and scientifically with children and the adults who bring them up and educate them, yet at the same time be accountable to society as a whole for the effectiveness, relevance and morality of their work.

Psychology is, and should be, primarily a scientific discipline. Whilst a psychologist may be guilty of unethical conduct if he conducts research that could be harmful to his subjects, he may be equally guilty of unethical conduct if he fails to conduct much needed research, particularly if he works in fields so characterised by ignorance that the systematic acquisition of knowledge is especially crucial (Haywood, 1976). The psychologist must therefore be in a position to be innovative in his work, and to expect innovation in the work of others, since without this potential for change he cannot be expected to translate demands for educational improvement into reality. Indeed without the possibility of change there appears to be little justification for employing psychologists at all. Therefore the first requirement for a practising developmental psychologist would be that he should be employed from the outset explicitly as a scientific researcher, but one whose research relates directly and concretely to practice (as indeed Burt was employed by the LCC, see Keir, op. cit.). Such work would inevitably involve the psychologist with individual children and their families, perhaps over protracted periods, so the second requirement would be that, within the restraints of the law, the psychologist should be free to establish relationships with his clients based on mutual trust and where appropriate act on his clients' behalf, even when this brought him into conflict with the immediate interests of his employing institution. To merit the responsibilities that stem from these two requirements psychologists would have to be accountable for maintaining the highest standards of professional conduct and technical expertise. The third requirement is therefore that the profession itself must not only ensure a high standard of directly relevant training, but also set and monitor subsequent professional standards to a level considerably above the level of the present postgraduate training courses.

Such a proposed developmental psychology profession therefore differs markedly, not only from the present professions of educational and clinical psychology, but also from the proposed child psychology profession (British Psychological Society, 1977) in prime purpose, in ethical status and in level of professional competence.

The initial recruits for such a group would inevitably be assembled on an *ad hoc* basis. Some would probably come from educational and clinical psychology, others from elsewhere in psychology, but from the outset the areas of their psychological contribution should be made explicit, a common syllabus for development and a common basic standard established. These should include competence in the social and sociological, the biological and medical factors that influence human mental development and behaviour, and legal, institutional, moral and philosophical aspects of child-rearing and education. Above all their contribution should relate to practice and to real social situations, and depend upon developmental and psychological models rather than on pathology. Presumably the British Psychological Society could monitor such a programme once established, but only an act of political will could bring it about.

The numbers of such psychologists need not be large, and the costs should be correspondingly low. Hopefully a few advantageously placed psychologists could bring greater social benefit than legions poorly placed. The tangible benefits from deploying psychologists in this manner are likely to be substantially greater than more-of-the-same psychological provisions on the present model.

There is a need for psychologists who are in a position to contribute evidence to public enquiries involving matters of psychological interest, so that the psychological aspects of problems of behaviour receive their due consideration. The major theoretical problems in the Colwell case, for example, have tended to be overshadowed by procedural matters (Howells, 1974). Similarly there is an urgent need for scientific evidence in the courts, to lift the general quality of reporting on developmental and behavioural matters, and psychology itself might benefit from the higher technical demands of being placed in an adversary position. And in an era of increasing pressure group politics psychology in this country ought to be in a position to test out its position on the advocacy of the needs of individual clients or client groups, the handicapped, children excluded from school, children in care, and so on. Medical specialisations such as paediatrics, otology and opthalmology require higher-level psychological input not only to those aspects of diagnosis and treatment where behaviour is an important factor, but also to as yet uninvestigated psychological sequelae of physical conditions. Above all there is need for an *independent* look at the relevance and effectiveness of our present child-rearing and educational institutions.

If such a professional group were to be established then training beyond a basic level would most appropriately be arranged in the field, on an apprenticeship basis as in the older professions of the law and medicine. Eligibility for promotion to the professionally autonomous grade (equivalent to a medical consultant) would depend upon the psychologist's demonstrating an appropriate level of skill and achievement at a personal and technical level though actual appointment would depend upon the employers. Court (1976) has suggested that further consideration should be given to organising psychological services independently of health, education or social services: perhaps such psychologists could depend upon public funds in a manner analogous to the arrangements made for general practitioners.

The continual aim of the new psychology profession should be to 'give itself away' in more than one sense. Not only should skills and insights gained in the work be continually passed on to others rather than reserved as the exclusive preserve of yet another psychological

helping profession, but there should be a general and constructive
demystification, defining the methods and the limits of what psychology
can do for those who use it. More especially, the effects of the psychological contribution should be closely monitored, not from within by
the professionals themselves, but independently, to assess its benefits
at both personal and social levels. Hopefully these might include the
emergence of a more robust psychology of childhood than we presently
possess, making more direct contribution to the processes of child-
rearing and education and significant extensions in the ways in which
psychology might be applied.

Proposing a 'new' psychological profession (albeit one with old
ideals) to explore questions of child development, upbringing and
education in a real-life setting poses the question of what to do with
the present educational psychology work force. The constraints and
restrictions placed upon the scientific potential of educational psychologists by their position as local government officers have denied
expression to the talent and goodwill that exist amongst their ranks, and
their general failure to date to deliver psychology to the schools should
not mask the real contribution that scientific findings and approaches
could already make to pedagogy. The profession of applied developmental psychologists suggested above offers one potential means
whereby psychology might be *practised* for the growing generation.
There remains the question of how psychology is to be *delivered,* particularly to our schools.
    Present school psychological services exist as a state within a state
in the educational system, separate from the schools that they serve,
and dependent upon central administration in their local education
authorities. They have their own internal hierarchies drawing professional time inevitably into 'administration', their own clerical services
and very often their own buildings. They exist as separate organisations
in an increasing 'network' (often in effect chaos) of help and support
services, so that co-operation, co-ordination, etc. are activities that
draw them further away from their prime function. Their separate existence is a contributory factor to the continuance both of the never-
ending 'referral' system, whereby attention is focused upon individual
children identified as problems, and of the false expectations, misunderstandings and suspicion that can occur between educational
psychologists and teachers as a result of their distant and superficial
interaction. It is true that educational psychologists will have themselves previously served as school teachers, but thereafter their training
and professional experience lie outside of the schools, and the contin-

gencies that contribute to their behaviour change along with their professional *locale*. The problem of delivering psychology into the schools for the benefit of all children, therefore, demands an organisational structure that eliminates the state within a state and makes for the maximal direct interaction between delivery system and recipients. And both as a psychological exercise and as an act of social policy it merits close evaluation.

The only place that this can be done is within the schools themselves. Present tendencies within education, in one dimension to co-ordinate the activities of pre-school, primary school and secondary school, in another to integrate schooling much more closely with 'the community', make this more feasible than it would have been only a few years ago. If indeed the schools in a given area do work much more closely as a unit, whatever the age group that they serve, in a closer and more meaningful relationship with their parents and other local institutions, then they offer a base for deploying educational psychologists in a context where their contribution could be put to the acid test of practice.

The Association of Educational Psychologists (op. cit.) has recently insisted most strongly that educational psychologists should have 'a firm foundation' within the educational system, and has proposed a target of one educational psychologist for every 5,000 children in England and Wales. But in every field our society is beginning to recognise that continuous growth is no longer inherently good, and that labour-intensive welfare provision must be visibly effective to justify itself. A school-based educational psychologist would certainly be as firmly founded in education as is possible. A secondary school, its feeder primary schools, the pre-school population in the area, and the special schools and other institutions serving that child population together would in most cases offer a psychologist-child ratio perhaps easier than 1:5,000. At the present national establishment of about 800 many such school groups would have to go unserved by an educational psychologist, offering the opportunity for a controlled evaluation. It should be noted that these would comprise no greater number of children than currently go without the service of an educational psychologist.

Having educational psychologists firmly rooted within a defined group of schools offers them real opportunities to demonstrate their contribution. It would enable them to relate directly to the pupils and teachers within their natural context, to experience the tensions and aspirations that exist within that context and to deliver their service with the minimum likelihood of misunderstanding. They would be clearly seen as related to the school system and would be in an advantageous position to work towards an explicit accountability and responsibility along with the schools as a whole. They could apply themselves closely to the problems of transfer from one level of education to the next and to the as yet unsettled question of the 'integration' of handicapped pupils. They could attend to the chaotic and unformulated area of 'pastoral care', and approach wider issues of organisation, management or curriculum than presently possible under the referral system. Their attachment to a specific geographical area would enable both a deeper appreciation of local issues relevant to their school group, and the understandings of child development and the effects of intervention that can come from following a defined population as it grows.

Such a redeployment creates no legal difficulties since educational psychologists are nowhere written into statute and their employment is wholly a matter of local discretion. The way has already been cleared for the transfer of educational psychologists (and other 'advisers') to a much closer relation to the teaching profession by the integration of their salary scale with that of the teachers. The abolition of their separate services would have the additional effects of freeing administrative educational psychologists for full-time professional work, and of freeing the local educational authorities from the expenditure required to maintain their separate buildings and clerical establishments.

Ultimately however, such an exercise is only justifiable by its effectiveness. At an immediate level evaluation would depend upon the face validity of the new service offered. In a closer proximity to the real problems of the schools the maintenance of credibility would be an immediate and continuous task. Different schools have to face very different problems, and educational psychologists have a variety of differing contributions to make. The 800 possible combinations should offer invaluable information on what sort of psychology, how delivered, has a beneficial influence upon such factors as school morale, pupil achievement, classroom behaviour, school attendance, special education provisions and so on, claimed by educational psychologists as their areas of practical expertise. The evaluation of the various matches of need to provision should not, of course, be conducted by educational psychologists themselves.

Educational psychologists, as presently recruited and trained, however they might be redeployed, do not present the only means whereby psychology may be delivered to the schools and to the wider education system. For example, Curr (1969) has argued that teachers without a first degree in psychology might, after a one-year course in child psychology, fulfil many of the functions presently undertaken by educational psychologists. Or perhaps attention to the structures and rewards that determine the behaviour of the teaching profession as a whole might have a more penetrating effect upon pedagogic practice and the degree to which it incorporates scientific methods and findings. Evaluation of educational psychologists' effectiveness as deliverers of psychology should also include critical comparison with such alternative delivery systems.

A redeployment and comparative evaluation of the nature proposed here offers educational psychologists an unprecedented opportunity to prove the effectiveness and benefit of the skills and services that they offer. It might be that as a result of such an exercise our society forms a most clear impression that an increase in the numbers of educational psychologists should be an important component of our economic preparations for the end of the century. On the other hand it is clear that some psychologists (or their psychologies) will show themselves inadequate to the task before them, and it is conceivable that the profession as a whole might fail to show worth. Should this be the case then the unneeded psychologists, all certificated teachers, might be reabsorbed into the school groups in which they have worked, in their previous role of schoolteachers.

Disruptions in professional practice need not be feared since they may lead to new ways of functioning not possible before. This is especially true in the case of psychology where the applied science is still too unsure of its precise nature to permit of its being prematurely frozen into particular organisational structures. The suggestions made here respond to the immediate contradictions inherent in the provision of the bulk of our developmental psychology *via* 'educational psychologists' who are neither wholly psychologists nor wholly educational. A profession of applied developmental psychologists of the kind suggested should make psychology more responsive to the demands of social reality both for the sake of the individual and of society: school-based educational psychologists should deliver psychology more directly to the 'chalk face' in the schools. If the two types of psychologist, or any other psychologists involved in child-rearing and education, should find themselves in an adversary position then perhaps all the better for the advance of psychology. If structural changes do succeed in bringing about technical changes, the measure of their significance will be social and political innovations following upon them. What happens to psychology then will be another matter.

The present 'energy crisis' does not really represent a shortage of energy, just a shortage of liquid hydrocarbons. The real crisis is the problem of how the abundance of energy available might be harnessed and equably distributed, this being partly a technical and partly a moral problem. Similarly the problem of how psychology might contribute positively to our future social needs does not represent a lack of talent, adaptable technique or good intention within psychology, but rather a failure to develop the structures whereby the potential of psychological science might be encouraged and permitted. Our children have a right to expect us to have tested out psychology to the full. Psychologists' present professionalism should not stand in the way of this.

THE PROCESS OF RECONSTRUCTION: AN
OVERVIEW

Gervase Leyden

The development of early psychological services and the work of educational psychologists in child guidance clinics has been fully documented
in Chapter 2 of the present volume and elsewhere (Keir, 1952;
Summerfield Report, Appendix A, 1968). It is clear from these
accounts that virtually from the outset most educational psychologists
were faced with a definition of their area of competence made by
other people. Burt (1969) in his review of the Summerfield Report,
quotes the views of Moodie (the first Medical Director of the first Child
Guidance Clinic) that 'psychology is a branch of knowledge dealing
with the structure and operation of intelligence; psychiatry is a branch
of medicine dealing with the mechanisms involved in all forms of behaviour, normal as well as abnormal'. With few exceptions this rele-
gated educational psychologists within child guidance clinics to a
psychometric role permitting occasional negotiation over the acceptability of personality testing and an occasional treatment session under
the guise of remedial work. Although psychologists sought to emerge
from this restricted role we absorbed many of those underlying clinical
assumptions to augment our heavily psychometric training.

One consequence of the early identification with child guidance and
perhaps the school health service, was that as psychologists we incorporated other assumptions into our work that were not necessarily
appropriate to psychological services. As a result we established the
concept of 'referrals', which related to 'children with problems', and
the referrals were generally initiated by someone other than the child or
his family. In turn this created 'waiting lists' before assessment or
'diagnosis' and occasionally 'treatment' could be attempted. Although
we followed medical concepts, we lacked the supportive resources,
staff and facilities those concepts imply. Schools must have been
relieved, if surprised, that a service was emerging to accept responsibility
for such assumptions. It is probably still true that schools do not
appreciate how meagre are the resources available to a school psychological service — particularly when it operates on a child guidance
model.

If the early psychological services had merely to work out the appropriateness of the medical assumptions alone, then subsequent developments might have been considerably more effective. However, many psychologists had received no formal training as educational psychologists, and a sizeable minority had not studied psychology at undergraduate level but had followed 'equivalent' higher degree courses, usually in education. Many had trained and worked as teachers before starting a study of psychology. When the information was collected for the Summerfield Report, 21 per cent of educational psychologists had taught for more than nine years, and a further 8 per cent for more than five years, but 40 per cent were without specific training in educational psychology, and 20 per cent had not studied psychology at undergraduate level. It is therefore hardly surprising that the early quest for a professional identity was also strongly influenced by assumptions deriving from a background in teaching, and the particular services of prescriptions and injunctions that this implied. What would have been the subsequent work had our introduction been as applied psychologists (even within the education service) but without a strong conceptual allegiance to other disciplines? Nevertheless the potential applied psychologist had first to resolve the dissonance between the clinical and educational assumptions before he could initiate ways of making his knowledge and skills available for the benefit of children and those responsible for them. In practice he found himself expected to offer both an individual or casework service for all children and their families who might be referred, as well as a support and advisory function for schools. This conflict could not be resolved effectively in those terms. Additional staff simply furnaced the latent demand, but the essential contradictions remained with the result that the recent improvements in staffing ratios have not alone been sufficient to settle the contradictions. Nor did the dramatic growth in school psychological services after the Second World War guarantee an independent profession. Many psychological services were administered by the school health service often with a corresponding limitation on role, although it is equally true that some services would not have been established without medical support. The 'range of duties' largely focused on psychometric assessment of individual children. Section 34 of the 1944 Education Act gave the local education authority the duty of ascertaining which children were in need of special educational treatment. The LEA was required to consider the advice of medical officers, together with reports from teachers and other persons. The information was summarised in a series of forms with the psychologist generally contributing little more than psychometric findings of ability and attainment to the medical form

2HP and the school medical officer making the actual educational recommendation. In the case of more severely handicapped children the psychologist was frequently not invited to contribute at all. Williams' (1965) article on the 'Ascertainment of ESN Children' is a good summary of the limitations of those procedures and of the arguments advanced by some psychologists for a more positive role.

The preoccupation with psychometry would not have survived for so long without nourishment from other sources, and this has been amply provided from within the profession. Most of the educational psychology training courses were based on the premise that assessment techniques were a major application of psychology to the problems of children. On my own training course I cannot recall seeing a child for any purpose other than to administer a test. Discussions about school organisation went little further than establishing whether they could provide an empty room for the psychologist and child. The development of 'prescriptive' tests only gave further support to the view that psychometry offered the most promising prospect. Few psychologists challenged Thorndike's dicta that 'If a thing exists, it exists in some amount' and 'if it exists in some amount, it can be measured'. Many in fact went further, 'If it can be measured, it should be measured'. The Psychologist's office became in Burt's phrase, 'an HQ for EQs and IQs'.

It must be difficult for recent entrants to the profession to appreciate the relatively uncritical enthusiasm for testing in the post-war years, and the unlikely situations in which it was practised. Cloakrooms, convents, assembly halls, dining rooms, prisons – even toilets, have featured in colleagues' accounts. I personally know of one psychologist whose practice was to test whoever was in the waiting room, whether he had been referred or not. Her subsequent reports contained fascinating allusions to the IQ and attainments of parents, relatives, neighbours – or whoever happened to accompany the child. Such mindless excess was a unique eccentricity but we did accept that individual assessment was a prime essential of our work. 'Diagnosis' was based on the knowledge of a wide range of tests and the ability to select the one most appropriate. Vernon (1968) was quite accurate in reflecting that 'the standard approach of British Child Psychologists when faced with a backward or maladjusted child, has been to test his IQ and attainments'.

Even on those limited terms few services, particularly in the Midlands and North could possibly cope with the demands on them. Most of the tests psychologists had been trained to use (e.g. WISC, ITPA, Griffiths, Merrill-Palmer) assumed individual work with children – and this was also the perspective of most training courses. Faced with school populations of 20,000 to 30,000 and a system of open referrals with no initial screening, the enthusiasm for testing began to wane, initially on the simple grounds that it was inappropriate and impossible for the large number of children referred. Psychology clearly had a relevance for many children, families, schools, in fact the whole community. But equally clearly the preparation of the educational psychologist and the assumptions of the school psychological service in which he worked obscured this.

In view of current psychological interest in the structure and organisation of schools it is ironic to recall the low priority given in the fifties and sixties (and alas, currently, in some services) to defining goals, evaluating procedures and providing support or opportunities for professional developments within our own services. Few professions at that time recognised the implications of the 'knowledge explosion' of the last few decades and 'preparation for change' was not an aspect of training courses. Although psychological services themselves were relatively new, as has been indicated their assumptions were more traditional. There was an understanding that the role of the psychologist was essentially static, gradually maturing and enriching in sophistication over time, a Stilton Cheese theory of role. Initially fresh and malleable, the psychologist soon achieves a firmness and even consistency which is quite palatable to most people. However, Dubin's work suggests that the 'shelf life' of the traditional product has significantly diminished over the years.

The rapid development of services in the 1950s produced expectations and demands from teachers and others that had not been entirely predicted. The introduction of a psychologist into an area previously without one did not simply graft an extra worker with a particular perspective into the old situation, but produced a totally fresh picture, revising the perceptions and expectancies of all the individuals, agencies and institutions with access to him. With an 'open' referral system this of course included everybody. It was at that point, faced with alarming and insistent demands for our time that we began to realise the irrelevance of many of our accumulated skills for the range of demands being made, particularly in view of the paltry support resources available. Doubts about the legitimacy of psychometry as practised were beginning to erode confidence in that technique. In addition clinical work was often criticised by teachers as remote and unrealistic. The response was a definite move from clinics to the setting where most of the referrals originated – the school. However, simply transferring 'individual assessments' or 'casework' from clinics to schools did not dispel those criticisms since the techniques themselves were of dubious relevance to the needs of the school as an institution and made little sense in the life of the pupils or teachers. The shift in premises was simply geographical.

Bruner (1966), in reviewing the failure of educational psychology to produce a major contribution to educational practice identified the basic flaw: *'the task was not really one of application in any obvious sense, but of formulation'*. Individual psychometry or treatment had not only failed to produce effective answers but prevented the appropriate questions being asked, since they had diverted the psychologist into a separate set of activities that were virtually self-contained – they asked their own questions and provided their own answers.

The reaction against the psychometric movement has been covered earlier in this book. It is too comfortable to forget that psychology departments and training courses endorsed the practice, and that the laudable intention was to identify and remedy children's learning difficulties. However the application of tests on the scale that we witnessed in the fifties and sixties had unintended results. Both child and psychologist were diminished by the process. The child became translated into a set of scores or numbers. (I worked in one service where all case notes had been filed in IQ categories.) His indifference, his anger, his confusion, his expectations, his fear were important to the extent that they were perceived to influence scores. The psychologist in turn was limited to a technician's role. Yet test scores did not provide explanations – they required them. Nevertheless as psychologists we frequently complied in using psychometric techniques to answer questions not formulated on educational, psychological or scientific grounds. For instance, group test surveys of school populations were regularly carried out to identify children for individual special school ascertainment. Far more time was allocated to this exercise than in asking questions about whether such children benefit from a separate form of education, or in studying the influence of school organisation of teaching methods on the failure of some children to progress in school. Perhaps the 'flooding' produced by the considerable period we spent questioning children overcame any tendency to ask questions elsewhere.

Clearly we were perceived by others, by teachers, parents, children, administrators and psychiatrists as psychometrists. Equally clearly we also saw this to be our area of particular competence and often operated entirely within this restricted framework. The reaction against psychometry induced further anxiety in those psychologists whose legitimacy pivoted on that technique, and there was no shortage of allusions to babies and bath water. Thus test scores provided an agenda for discussion in which neither teacher nor psychologist felt threatened and the search for explanation by tacit agreement focused in the child's responses. Take that away, and where might it lead? Even Burden's (1973) recent indictment of current tests hedges at the point of implementing his own conclusions, and is tantalisingly vague about alternatives and how they might be introduced.

Fortunately it is impossible to follow any work with pupils, teachers or parents in schools without being made forcibly aware of the significance of school organisation, the internal social dynamics, the curriculum — and the status accorded to different parts of it, and even the extent to which the design of the buildings can impose its own pattern on the structure of the school day. Although the same traditional techniques were initially applied the perspective rapidly broadened to encompass not only an individual child but also other contributory factors from within the school itself. Once this point was reached, the sterility of the traditional approach became obvious and the process of reformulation inevitable. Suddenly it became permissible and necessary to exorcise other inherited shibboleths which influenced the way in which we were working.

During the 1960s there was a decisive shift away from testing for the purpose of classifying, towards assessment as a basis for consequent remediation for the child or the situation. Inevitably this stimulated a re-examination of our role in ascertaining children for ESN(M) schools. For many years this had been an issue where the dissonance between the medical and educational elements was resolved, and for once the precarious trick of riding both horses simultaneously seemed relevant beyond the circus ring. 'Disability of mind' required 'special educational treatment'. There was a general consensus among educational psychologists in the fities and sixties that the responsibility for making such judgements should not rest with school medical officers, but that psychologists and teachers should be primarily involved (Woods, 1975; Williams, 1965).Eventually these views were recognised by Circular 2/75 which outlined the essential psychological contribution in identifying children's needs and suggested some improved procedures for recording them. Ironically, these were introduced after a decade during which the concept of segregated special schooling had been seriously questioned. Circular 2/75 did not explicitly acknowledge these misgivings, but the wording of the new procedures does permit the alternative use of special resources.

The controversy in the 1960s about the value and implications of separate special education echoed the heredity/environment debate. Post-war, the ESN category unwittingly was more akin to a medical/ educational condition. As previously indicated, the official 2HP was headed 'Report on child examined for a disability of mind'. It concluded that the child 'is/is not' educationally subnormal with a caveat for those children 'unsuitable for education at school' and children requiring a special physical examination or treatment at a child guidance clinic. The hereditarian-constitutional argument held sway. The psychologist contributed little more than IQ or other test scores for the medical officer to include under the 2HP, although even here some doctors carried this out themselves.

Yet the link between educational failure and social or cultural factors had been well established as far back as Gordon's studies of canal boat children in the 1920s, and had been freshly emphasised by the Newsom and Plowden reports and by research studies into the effectiveness of compensatory programmes. Evaluation studies of special schooling proved disturbing. Williams and Gruber (1967) classified the environmental handicaps suffered by children in ESN schools and found reduced infant schooling (as with summer born children) to be an important school variable associated with educational failure. Certainly no evidence emerged that the children attending ESN schools were a homogeneous group, but in fact encompassed a broad range of social handicap and learning difficulties. The grouping was primarily administrative and gave no indication of need, nor did it prescribe programmes or methods of teaching. In view of the diversity of 'diagnosis', it is not surprising to find that research evidence of the value of special schooling is, at best, inconclusive. Tizard (1966), whilst acknowledging the limitations of most of the evaluation studies, was only able to identify one such investigation which indicated clear cut gains by children receiving special schooling — and this was in a special class. Numerous other studies found no actual gains, and evidence that some children did less well. More recent reviews of evaluation research on special schooling (Presland, 1970; Moseley, 1975; Morgan, 1977; Ghodsian and Calnan, 1977) have not been able to present conclusive evidence of its effectiveness on the criteria studied, although it is possible there may be improved personal and social adjustment within the school in some cases. However, there is a strong risk that the children may have a difficulty in integrating within the community and in adjusting to an adult role and job. Many of the studies can be criticised precisely on the grounds that these sort of difficulties led to the original placement in a special school, but this does not answer the criticism that there seems to be little positive evidence that schools have been successful in helping children to overcome their difficulties. That so little evidence exists, and that so much of it is inconclusive is not a criticism of the work of special schools, nor of teachers. It is a further sad demonstration that as educational psychologists we have tended to accept assumptions without testing them, and have not rigorously scrutinised our own work. The hours spent in 'routine ascertainment' were in inverse proportion to the fleeting evaluation of the merit of what was being done.

This position has uneasy ethical overtones for the psychologist in his work with individual children and parents. In the light of current evidence, how do we answer parents' anxieties or children's fear of stigma if special schooling is proposed? Nor do those occasions where parent and child express no reservation necessarily justify such a move. Miller (1973) represented the views of a number of psychologists: 'Separating children from their peers, labelling them as deficient, and inadequate, and denying their parents rights over choice of schooling is a fairly drastic procedure. In order for it to be justified, the evidence that children benefit from the process must be unequivocal, and obvious not only to the teachers and administrators, but to the parents and children themselves. This evidence appears to be lacking.'

An appreciation of a child's educational development clearly involves a study of the interaction between the child and his school. Similarly, there is an inter-relationship between ESN(M) schools and their feeder primary and secondary schools. The special schools have played an essentially passive role in receiving children referred to them, via the school and psychological service, as 'slow learners'. In practice the referral was often triggered by the child presenting management difficulties in the school, of which learning difficulties were only a part. Consequently special schools have been faced with a significant number of children presenting both learning and behaviour problems and this in turn has required the school to devise methods of coping with their additional needs. The school cannot proceed on the premise that its pupils are primarily experiencing learning difficulties and that emotional or social problems are little more common than in other schools. Furthermore, the actual existence of special schools influences the outlook and organisation of its feeders, particularly in respect of slow learning children. Faced with unresponsive and possibly 'difficult' pupils and the knowledge that a system of special schools exists it is not surprising that the latter are often seen as an answer. When acute educational failure can be resolved by transferring the failing pupil to a special school, a valuable feedback function may be lost. The original school may lose the incentive to examine the role of its own organisation and methods in contributing to what is seen simply as a child's failure. Nor does it encourage the school to consider ways in which additional resources of staff, equipment and guidance can combine to provide an appropriate learning and developmental climate for the child in his own school. Responsibility for the acutely failing child is transferred from the feeder to the special school. The psychologist acts merely as catalyst in this process, absolving himself even from the responsibility of evaluating the changes he has engineered.

One of the dangers of the institutional role of the educational psychologist is that the apparent client may be contaminated by the institutional client. Although the apparent client may be a child experiencing difficulties, the covert client is often the institution, be it school or authority. Removal of this 'problem' from the jurisdiction of the institution may be interpreted as success. Such a crude oversimplification clearly ignores some essential factors of the situation, such as individual successes achieved by special schools, difficulties of reallocating resources for an individual child at local level, and it also denies the genuine concern and skilled help demonstrated by individual teachers. Nevertheless, the psychologist has to take into account and understand the influence of institutional forces — particularly if they run counter to the needs of the child.

Although most of the studies cited offer little support for current practices in segregated special schooling, there is evidence that 'compensatory' methods based on careful diagnosis of individual needs and subsequent 'prescriptive' programmes can be effective. The work of Morgan (1971; see also Moseley, 1975) at Dinsdale Park School is one of the more impressive demonstrations of how individually structured learning programmes can overcome reading difficulties in disadvantaged, slow learning children. Now that the administrative category of ESN pupils is beginning to give way to individual identification of need, it should be possible to study more effective ways of allocating resources for special education. If the needs are social or cultural, then education ought to reflect this and the research projects in compensatory education in both this country and abroad should be studied, if only to avoid the well-documented mistakes. For smaller groups of children who are experiencing more specific learning difficulties there are promising implications in the work of both Schubert (1973) and Wedell

(1973). Such approaches may in fact demonstrate a continuing need for some form of special schools as a 'learning resource' not for children broadly categorised as 'ESN' but for those whose learning difficulties require more sophisticated analysis and remedial techniques.

I have given some attention to the issue of special schooling because it seems to me that the psychologist's contribution to it offers some immediate lessons about our services and the way we work. Initially we contributed largely as psychometrists, as technicians, providing test scores for other people to use. It would be naive to assume that individuals did not circumvent this, but most of us did not make a full contribution as psychologists, and were not always able to control the way in which our findings were implemented. For instance, a recommendation for special education could be interpreted in various ways by the school, teacher, psychologist, adviser or medical officer. In cases where actual placement was decided by administrators there was no guarantee that the education provided would match the needs of the child as defined. More currently, 'giving psychology away' clearly requires a greater responsibility for the psychologist in being aware of the situation in which it is being used, in monitoring and perhaps controlling that usage. (And at that point it can hardly be called a gift!)

The dearth of research on the value of special school placement is a rebuke to the psychologists who initiated such recommendations, not to the teachers involved. Where services are too busy or overwhelmed to evaluate their recommendations then there are more dangers in continuing uncritically than in calling a halt for an appraisal of what is being achieved and what is being assumed. Unguided activity does not confer effectiveness and surely we no longer have to justify the need for services to create time for identifying objectives and goals, devising and evaluating methods of achieving them and permitting staff opportunities for developing their own professional skills.

All these lessons apply equally to our work in child guidance clinics. The traditional model of psychiatrist, psychiatric social worker and psychologist working as an interdisciplinary team gave the psychologist in training and in practice the chance to play a role in treatment. Seldom the lead, it did sometimes include lines, but was generally little more than a walk on part. The audience though small, was loyal, middle-class and prepared to queue at length for a production which achieved a lengthy run before the critics gave it their serious attention. Using a terminal metaphor, Rehin's (1972) article 'Child Guidance at the end of the Road' charged clinics with operating an obsolete Freudian methodology whose effectiveness they have not been able to

demonstrate. He rejected the 'team' concept as being a wasteful dupli-
cation of scarce resources and offering virtually no role for the father, a
striking anomaly where the focus is the whole family rather than the
child alone. Some of Rehin's assumptions about treatment and the concept of 'mental illness' failed to register the particular disenchantment
with child guidance felt by many practitioners and clients. However, his
criticisms of the highly selective intake, irrational referrals and the use
of highly educated, high status professions on an exercise of unproven
value available only to a small fraction of the child population
expressed fairly widespread misgivings. Although Rehin rejected the
current practice of child guidance on the grounds of ineffectiveness and
theoretical inadequacy, his proposals concerned themselves with the
administrative reconstruction of health, educational and social services
rather than the helping process itself. Tizard (1973) similarly found
little evidence that child guidance as a clinical activity was appropriate
for the size or nature of difficulties experienced by children and
families in the community. However he suggested a more limited,
clearly specified approach to treatment, with the actual emphasis of the
service shifting to school-based measures. Although child guidance
clinics had focused on the child as a symptom of the family problem,
Tizard was urging a broader perspective to include the social environment of the school as a contributor to the incidence and duration of
'maladjusted' behaviour. Although individual clinic teams essayed into
schools. Tizard's conclusions did not reflect a concerted trend in child
guidance practice away from a preoccupation with child pathology.
Indeed, following Rehin, most of the debate has been concerned with
where the clinic team members should be based, rather than what they
should do. Whether or not child guidance clinics reappraise their purpose
and practice, the role of the educational psychologist within such teams
needs rescuing from its archaic obsolescence. The role advocated by
Tizard recognises the recent developments in psychological services and
a renewed interest in the application of psychological theory to work
with children. Unless the teamwork principle permits each member an
effective contribution it is not worth upholding. If developments in
child guidance practice and philosophy over the next few years recognise and incorporate the full potential of each contributor a different
and possibly exciting and effective interdisciplinary service may emerge.
Not all the regional discussions following Circular 3/74 and its proposals
of 'a network of services' engender optimism, but there is still time for a
productive realignment. If not, then Olive Sampson's (1975) article 'A
dream that is dying?' may have sounded the lament.

Hindsight too easily passes as insight and facile criticism of traditional practice often reveals a lack of appreciation of constraints imposed on developing services. It was not the purpose of local authorities to provide general employment for educational psychologists, and services were generally introduced by education departments with certain tasks in mind, and with their own assumptions about how such tasks might be carried out. The last fifteen years have been a painful struggle to reappraise those functions and only by so doing has it been possible to emerge from a hybrid teacher-clinician role to that of psychologist, based in the education service. The point at which schools, or other agencies, feel it worthwile to *invite in* a psychologist to provide an additional perspective or help them overcome a problem rather than *referring on* a child gives the school access to a far wider range of alternatives. These can also include the possibility of individual help for the child if appropriate.

This sort of development has been hindered by the rather inflexible use of referral forms by both teachers and psychologists. The principle of open referrals was laudable, but the form itself had some undesirable connotations, and obscured the issue of who was the real client. Interestingly enough when parents or pupils spontaneously sought the help of a psychologist they were not asked to complete such a form. While forms remain in use, Hedderly's (1976) advocacy of a contract-based referral system indicates that services can adopt a more flexible policy. However, there is a clear need for some post-Caxton innovations to improve the communication between psychological services and those who use them. Perhaps some of the confusion surrounding the debate on the use of referral forms relates to the broader issue of the extent to which the psychologist undertakes any individual work with children — or whether he intervenes solely at the individual level. In my view this is a false choice. School organisation and curriculum matters cannot be seen in isolation from the individual child any more than the child can be divorced from his social or school setting. The dilemma is in being available to those children or families who may be significantly helped (however defined) by the intervention of a psychologist, without being submerged under a confetti of forms. A large part of the solution is to work with and through the institution and as this is at the expense of time traditionally spent on individual work it is even more important that those cases selected for individual study or casework are carefully and effectively identified. Unfortunately, many referrals are not appropriate and too much time is spent by psychologists in 'personal screening' usually by a school visit. Increasing the information content (and researching the validity) of the referral process may reduce this, but progress ultimately depends on the recognition that 'referral forms' of 'problem children' are not the only means of initiating discussion between teachers and psychologists. Furthermore, it would be interesting to study the implications of limiting actual individual casework or intervention to those children or families who refer themselves, rather than to focus so heavily on those who are referred by someone else.

In fact, most services would be hard pressed to offer an adequate individual face-to-face service for 5 per cent of the school population, and would be utterly swamped if 10 per cent were referred. Yet the evidence of the Isle of Wight Survey and the National Children's Bureau indicates that a significantly higher proportion present problems of educational concern. Even if intervention on traditional lines were an appropriate response, only one or two services in this country are currently staffed at a sufficient level to be able to offer it, and even these services would question the assumptions behind mass referrals for some form of 'psychological' screening. Clearly we should reserve individual case studies for those situations where the focus of the problem is both 'within' the child or family and amenable to such techniques. With a more selective referral procedure, it would then be possible for services to offer teachers and others more guidance and support in overcoming difficulties in the setting where they occur, be it in school, home or elsewhere. Although one could make a case that all school children would benefit from individual face-to-face guidance by an educational psychologist, this is not currently feasible — nor is it necessary if closer liaison between psychologists and teachers permits primary help to be offered to all children through the teacher.

Where have these developments led us? If Toffler's 'future shock' is the realisation that the world you have been trained to believe in does not exist, then there are some advanced cases within the psychological services. Educational psychologists of my generation and older have found the basic tenets of a significant part of our training and practice increasingly open to question from ourselves and others. The pace of dissatisfaction may have accelerated, but the embryonic doubts themselves have been present for the last fifteen years or so. The Summerfield Report (1968), following up migrants from the profession, found pressure of work together with reservations about the quality and usefulness of some of it were already being advanced — along with misperceptions of role and problems of communication with medical and

administrative colleagues. Such studies as are available have only confirmed those doubts, and we have now reached a stage where a rethinking and reformulating of the function of psychological services is
inevitable, if only because so many of the traditional assumptions no
longer hold. The most hopeful sign is that the critical rethinking is not
the sole prerogative of new entrants to the profession and that much of
the thrust is from those trained in conventional lines who have
attempted to implement that training. In the past decade there has been
a counter growth of spontaneous innovations by individual services and
individual psychologists. Doubts about the uncritical use of norm-
referenced tests, the process of selecting children for special schooling
and our work in child guidance clinics have been voiced loudly within
the profession. Most of the subsequent innovations have taken as their
theme a more flexible dialogue and openness between psychologists and
consumers and less reliance on professional mysteries, relics and rituals,
counterpointed by research or evaluation of the measures. Thus,
although these developments are not centrally orchestrated they are
forming a recognisable movement.

   The development of school-based measures and various kinds of
teachers' courses or 'workshops' signalled the shift of emphasis away
from responding to individual referrals towards experimenting with preventive measures. Initially courses tended to be a simple extension of
the limited role previously outlined, and were largely restricted to such
topics as educational testing or reading failure. By the late 1960s a
number of services had developed a variety of integrated measures such
as residential courses, supportive pamphlets and information sheets,
and school-based experiments in alternative ways of meeting the needs
of special groups of pupils. For example, the West Sussex service under
Labon (Labon, 1973; Acklaw and Labon, 1971) was one of a number
which explored what could be achieved by attempting to apply psychological concepts to 'problem areas' within schools — as well as developing a comprehensive network of courses and discussions with
teachers on other educational issues. An important element in the West
Sussex service was the allocation of time for the psychologist to update
his own knowledge and skills, and this was a further sign of the profession beginning to respond to its changing role. Also at this time Presland
(1970, 1973, 1975) began his series of pamphlets for teachers in which
he gave highly practical examples of how a range of psychological techniques could be applied to the sort of difficulties faced by class
teachers. Another recent example is the work of Wolfendale (1976) in
developing a screening procedure that was essentially a feedback device

for teachers linked to in-service training and the production of
materials.

Courses have now become a commonplace for making psychological
findings available not only to teachers, but also to parents, social
workers, residential staff and others, and videotape recording techniques have proved particularly appropriate for this work.
Encouragingly, the preparation of in-service courses for teachers and
others is now being included in some training courses for psychologists
(Ward, 1975). The need to improve pre-crisis contact has become
generally established. However, as most educational issues are multi-
dimensional, other agencies such as advisers and college education
departments also have a significant contribution to make; we should
jointly aim for a colloquium rather than a bilateral dialogue.

This greater emphasis on courses and workshops has been one extension of role, and has demonstrated that the psychologist can be an
appropriate consultant or facilitator to whom teachers and parents can
turn. The possibilities of such contacts transcend the alleviation of
'problems', and the workshop approach, particularly with parents of
handicapped children has produced highly encouraging results. A major
advantage of joint workshops is that the psychologist-client/parent
relationship is avoided and this permits few more challenging discussions
and feedback. This can spark off a more creative fusion, of which one
example is the Cleveland parent-psychological service group. Originally
this grew from a series of joint film seminars between psychologists and
parents in touch with the psychological service but grew into a more
broadly based parent group, supported by the psychologists who acted
as facilitators within the group, and for the group within the local
authority. This generated a whole range of specialist resources including
a Toy Library, Parent Workshop, weekend use of swimming pools for
handicapped children and their families, film seminars, Saturday
morning and school holiday playgroups, all developed against a
background of discussion about children's and families' needs. This was
a remarkable achievement within just two years and illustrates what is
possible when the psychologist steps beyond the restrictions of a purely
clinical role and risks himself and his professional skills by joining with
parents or others in the process of defining and attaining their goals.

If individual casework alone does not offer a sufficiently productive
support for schools (and is only available to a small proportion of
children, given current staffing levels), where should we concentrate our
relatively limited resources in order to offer a more effective service?
There seems little doubt that the school curriculum, organisation and

the need to offer staff more personal guidance and support in their pastoral work are vital areas. The Newsom and Plowden reports (and to an extent, Bullock) created an atmosphere in which some refreshing developments took place, particularly in terms of the curriculum. Our interest should certainly not be confined to the areas of reading, or particular learning difficulties, and Bruner's 'Man: A Course of Study' (MACOS) is an ambitious illustration of what can be achieved. 'A' level psychology courses are also on the syllabus of some schools, and others have introduced option courses in child development with the local psychological service (and the next generation of parents). Certainly one of the advantages of working with individuals or groups of pupils is that it provides an insight into the meaning of the whole school day from their point of view, and the extent to which the curriculum reflects their personal, social and intellectual needs. It reminds us that at all ages and stages of schooling many classroom problems relate primarily to the gap between the child and the extent to which the tasks he is set are relevant to him at this stage of his growth and are within his competence to perform. My own teaching (innocent of Newsom) contained quaint but largely irrelevant vignettes on such topics as 'A day in the life of a lumberjack' or 'Hop pickers in Kent' to adolescents who needed more direct guidance in making sense of their own society and their own behaviour. If we are genuinely concerned about such issues as vandalism in schools, relationships with young people and preparation for life in a broader community, then many elements of the overt curriculum still seem bizarre.

In respect of school organisation and the need to offer more support particularly to pastoral care and other specialist staff, we have been surprisingly reluctant to grasp the positive opportunities. Nevertheless as we are concerned with the personal growth and development of pupils – and not 'merely' their academic attainments – we do have a distinct contribution to the organisation and functioning of school pastoral care systems. It is an increasingly common experience that a more productive impact can be made by joining in with school-based meetings of pastoral care tutors and their relevant staff, both in terms of discussions of the needs of specific children as well as in considering (and evaluating) the effects of school-based procedures on the adjustment and development of the pupils. This approach does not preclude further individual work with some children any more than a 'child-focused' perspective would ignore the social and family context, but it does mean that any subsequent intervention with individuals or small groups is likely to be more effective if backed up by a network of in-school support systems, which of course are also available to all pupils, and not just those few whom the psychologist can help directly.

What other assistance can we offer schools in this area? In-service workshops and courses have already been advocated, and joint exercises of this kind which explore the growth process and are perhaps less didactic will benefit both teachers and psychologists. More formally, schools do need more evidence on which to make decisions about organisation, care systems and remedial arrangements. Secondary schools in particular have faced difficult decisions during the past decade as they have been internally reorganised and often regrouped. Yet at the time such decisions were being taken Weeks (1966) was pointing out 'the only experience we really have of such large institutions is the older public schools, the lunatic asylums and Her Majesty's prisons'. However the need for continued research at local level is underlined by Galloway's (1976) recent intriguing survey of Sheffield schools which found no evidence that large schools had a higher truancy rate or excluded more pupils. Projects of this nature seem a fruitful area of joint enquiry by schools and psychological services. There is a clear need for some careful evaluation of the effects of different forms of school measures on the adjustment, development and progress of pupils, to be carried out within authorities to provide local answers to questions since neighbourhood and other community factors can impose their own imprint on what is feasible.

If then we are to offer both a sophisticated casework in respect of the most complex client-centred problems and also function as an effective up-to-date psychological resource to whom teachers and others can turn, our own in-service or part experience training is in urgent need of development. Some services already make internal arrangements of this nature (e.g. Cleveland, Nottinghamshire) but there are many reasons why it should be extended. For instance, a significant number of practising educational psychologists were trained according to concepts that are no longer widely held. Apart from the annual DECP courses there have been relatively few opportunities for psychologists to update skills. A further consequence of the growth of psychological knowledge and research into child development is the demands this imposes on the individual psychologist faced with a wide range of duties and requests for help. Can one person bring equivalent expertise to studies of a pre-school blind child; a gifted sixth former who becomes seriously depressed; or a hyperactive seven-year-old presenting severe management problems in an open plan school? Faced with such a range of complexity, I am sure that many psychologists did fall back on tests in an attempt to make sense of an apparently bewildering case load. As Cornwall (1973) remarked, 'It would be difficult to imagine the individual who had the requisite knowledge, interest and aptitude to meet the demands made at every age and ability level. All this provides a strong argument, at a time when change is imminent, and at a time when we are in a position to determine how our professional role will develop, to consider the implications of specialisation for professional practice and structure.' Cornwall lists nine areas of specialism (e.g. pre-school children, reading disability, counselling, research, children with specific handicaps, etc.) and discusses ways in which they might be incorporated within the structure of a service. Specialist posts require advanced post-experience training and this would probably be more appropriately based within university training departments where particular specialisms currently exist. However, the continuing in-service training previously advocated could properly be based within the local authority service, perhaps with a regional pooling of internal resources as well as link-ups with existing training departments.

In view of the changes we have witnessed over the past decade, and the likelihood that the pace of change will accelerate, a commitment to a systematic, continuous programme of in-service training for psychologists is more important than ever if we are to adopt a responsible approach to our clients and offer 'value for money' to the local authority which employs us. The past decade has also seen an unusually large influx of new entrants to the profession, and this in a sense has disseminated the fruits of current training throughout the profession to an extent that is unlikely to be repeated as economic cut-backs and the effects of the falling birth rate reduce the number of places on training courses. Not all the suggested innovations have proved feasible or appropriate, but they have served as a catalyst and as a result provoked other developments. The examples given in the latter half of this chapter are particularly interesting to me as they illustrate what can be achieved within the existing structure of services, quite apart from the more revolutionary developments discussed in earlier chapters.

In Bruner's terms, we are making the decisive step from 'application' to 'formulation' and regardless of the particular path taken, the role has changed for all time. The ground clearing of the last five to ten years has made it possible for growth to occur at the level of both infrastructure and superstructure so there are unusual opportunities for development across age levels and hierarchies. Dare we take it — and the responsibility of defining what we mean and what we contribute as psychologists? Or will we remain content in our discontent, forever attributing our condition to the restrictions we perceive to be imposed on us by others?

REFERENCES

Addison, R.M. and Homme, L.E. (1966) The reinforcing event menu. *National Society for Programmed Instruction Journal, 5,* 8-9.

Acklaw, J. and Labon, D. (1971) School-based therapy: a pilot scheme. *Journal of the Association of Educational Psychologists. 2* (10), 35-9.

Allport, G. (1937) *Personality: A Psychological Interpretation.* New York: Holt, Rinehart and Winston.

Archibald, W.P. (1976) Psychology, sociology and social psychology: bad fences make bad neighbours. *British Journal of Sociology. 172,* 115-29.

Association of Educational Psychologists (1976) *Psychological Services for Local Authorities.* (Revised edition) Durham: AEP.

Bandura, A. and Walters, R.H. (1963) *Social Learning and Personality Development.* New York: Holt, Rinehart and Winston.

Barker, R.G. (1968) *Ecological Psychology.* California: Stanford University Press.

Becker, H.S. (1966) *Outsiders.* New York: The Free Press.

Beishon, J. and Peters, G. (1972) *Systems Behaviour.* London: Harper and Row for the Open University.

Bell, R.Q. (1968) A re-interpretation of the direction of effects in studies of socialisation. *Psychological Review. 75,* 81-95.

Bender, M.P. (1976) *Community Psychology.* London: Methuen.

Bloom, B.S. (1964) *Stability and Change in Human Characteristics.* New York: Harcourt, Brace and World.

Bowlby, J. (1975) *Separation: Anxiety and Anger.* Harmondsworth: Penguin Books.

Brim, O.G., Jr, Crutchfield, R.S. and Holtzman, W.H. (1966). *Intelligence: Perspectives 1965.* New York: Harcourt, Brace and World.

Brindle, P. (1974) The assessment of mild subnormality in education. Unpublished M.Ed. (Ed. Psych.) Dissertation: University of Birmingham.

British Psychological Society (1976) Consultation paper on training in child psychology. London: BPS Professional Affairs Board.

Bruner, J.S. (1966) *Towards a Theory of Instruction.* New York: Norton.

Burden, R.L. (1973) If we throw the tests out of the window what is there left to do? *Journal of the Association of Educational Psycho-*

logists. 3 (5), 6-9.

Burden, R.L. (1974) Teaching teachers about reading problems: the need for involvement at every level. *Remedial Education. 9* (3), 132-4.

Burden, R.L. (1976) Training educational psychologists to work in schools: the Exeter approach. *Remedial Education. 11* (2), 61-8.

Burt, C. (1947) *Mental and Scholastic Tests.* (3rd edition) London: Staples Press.

Burt, C. (1957) *The Causes and Treatment of Backwardness.* (4th edition) London: University of London Press.

Burt, C. (1964) The school psychological service: its history and development. Address to the 1st. Annual Conference of the Association of Educational Psychologists.

Burt, C. (1969) Psychologists in the education services. *Bulletin of the British Psychological Society. 22,* 1-11.

Chazan, M., Moore, T., Williams, P. and Wright, H.J. (1974) *The Practice of Educational Psychology.* London: Longman.

Cicourel, A.V. (1968) *The Social Organization of Juvenile Justice.* New York: John Wiley; re-issued 1976, London: Heinemann.

Committee on Child Health Services (1976) *Fit for the Future.* (The Court Report). London: HMSO.

Community Relations Commission (1977) A note on the Race Relations Act 1976 for Local Authorities. London: CRC.

Cooper, P. (1975) Social service departments' observation and assessment centres for children. *MOPP Discussion Paper No. 3.* Birmingham: Movement of Practising Psychologists.

Cornwall, K.F.C. (1973) Post-experience training and specialisation. Paper presented to DECP conference on training, June 1973.

Crane, A.R. (1959) An historical and critical account of the accomplishment quotient idea. *British Journal of Educational Psychology. 29,* 252-9.

Cronbach, L.J. (1970) *Essentials of Psychological Testing.* New York: Harper and Row.

Crowley, R.H. (1936) The problem of the backward child. Address presented to the Conference of the National Union of Teachers. London: NUT.

Cummings, J.D. (1944) The incidence of emotional symptoms in school children. *British Journal of Educational Psychology. 14,* 151-61.

Cummings, J.D. (1946) A follow-up study of emotional symptoms in school children. *British Journal of Educational Psychology. 16,* 163-77.

Curr, W. (1969) Critical notice on 'Psychologists in Education Services' (The Summerfield Report). *British Journal of Educational Psychology.* 39, 92-6.

Davie, R. (1976) Children and families with special needs. *Journal of the Association of Educational Psychologists. 4* (1), 1-9.

Department of Education and Science (1968) *Psychologists in Education Services* (The Summerfield Report). London: HMSO.

Department of Education and Science (1975) The discovery of children requiring special education and the assessment of their needs: *Circular 2/75.* London: HMSO.

Department of Education and Science (1975) *Educational Priority: Vol. 4: The West Riding Project.* London: HMSO.

Dessent, T. (1976) Some alternative approaches in educational psychology: an interview study. Unpublished M.A. project: University of Nottingham.

Downs, A. (1971) Decision making in bureaucracy. In: F.G. Castles, D.J. Murray and D.C. Potter (eds) *Decisions, Organisations and Society.* Harmondsworth: Penguin Books.

Downing, J. and Thackray, D. (1971) *Reading Readiness.* London: University of London Press.

Dubin, S.S. (1974) The psychology of lifelong learning. New developments in the professions. *International Review of Applied Psychology. 23* (1), 17-30.

Edwards, C. (1972) WISC and Witchy Poo. *Remedial Education. 7* (1), 20-21.

Elliott, C. (1976) Let's monitor standards in schools. *Education.* (3 Sept.) 189-90.

Erikson, K.T. (1962) Notes on the sociology of deviance. *Social Problems. 9,* 307-14.

Evans, R. (1975) Scientific or scientistic? *Journal of the Association of Educational Psychologists. 3* (8), 16-19.

Eysenck, H.J. (1969) The technology of consent. *New Scientist.* (26 June), 688-714.

Finlayson, D. *et al.* (1971) *Teacher Questionnaire on School Goals Questionnaire.* Slough: NFER.

Frankl, V.E. (1973) *Psychotherapy and Existentialism.* Harmondsworth: Penguin Books.

Frostig, M. and Horne, D. (1964) *The Frostig Program for the Development of Visual Perception.* Chicago: Follett.

Galloway, D.M. (1976) Size of school, socio-economic hardship, suspension rates and persistent unjustified absence from school. *British*

Journal of Educational Psychology. 46 (1), 40-47.

Ghodsian, M. and Calnan, M. (1977) A comparative longitudinal analysis of special education groups. *British Journal of Educational Psychology. 47* (2), 162-74.

Gillham, W.E.C. (1974) The British Intelligence Scale: à la recherche du temps perdu. *Bulletin of the British Psychological Society. 27*, 307-12.

Gillham, W.E.C. (1975) Educational psychology. In: W.E.C. Gillham (ed.) *Psychology Today.* London: Hodder and Stoughton/Teach Yourself Books.

Gillham, W.E.C. (1975) Intelligence: the persistent myth. *New Behaviour. 1* (10), 26 June.

Gillham, W.E.C. (1978) Measurement constructs and psychological structure. In: J. Radford and A. Burton (eds) *Perspectives on Thinking.* London: Methuen.

Giorgi, A. (1969) Psychology: a human science. *Social Research. 36,* 412-32.

Georgiades, N.J. (1975) Myths, dragons and behavioral scientists. Paper presented at the Center for Creative Leadership, Greenboro, North Carolina.

Georgiades, N.J. and Phillimore, L. (1975) The myth of the hero-innovator and alternative strategies for organizational change. In: C.C. Kiernan and F.P. Woodford (eds) *Behaviour Modification with the Severely Retarded.* Amsterdam: Associated Scientific Publishers.

Glaser, R. (1973) Educational psychology and education. *American Psychologist. 28,* 557-66.

Goldstein, H. and Blinkhorn, S. (1977) Monitoring educational standards— an inappropriate model. *Bulletin of the British Psychological Society. 30,* 309-11.

Guttman, L. (1971) Measurement as structural theory. *Psychometrika. 36,* 329-48.

Hargreaves, D.H. (1967) *Social Relations in a Secondary School.* London: Routledge and Kegan Paul.

Hargreaves, D.H. (1971) The delinquent subculture and the school. In: W.G. Carson and P. Wiles (eds) *Crime and Delinquency in Britain.* London: Robertson.

Hargreaves, D.H., Hester, S.K. and Mellor, F.J. (1975) *Deviance in Classrooms.* London: Routledge and Kegan Paul.

Hargreaves, D.H. (1976) The interactionist approach to deviance — some implications for educational psychologists. *MOPP Discussion Paper No. 10.*

Hawks, D.V. (1971) Can clinical psychology afford to treat the individual? *Bulletin of the British Psychological Society. 24,* 133-5.

Haywood, H.C. (1976) The ethics of doing research . . . and of not
doing it. *American Journal of Mental Deficiency. 81* (4), 311-17.

Hearnshaw, L.S. (1964) *A Short History of British Psychology.* London:
Staples Press.

Hedderly, R. (1976) The Development of a contract-based referral
system. Paper presented to a meeting of the Northern Branch of the
DECP.

Herbert, G.W. (1973) Educational psychologists in practice. *Bulletin of
the British Psychological Society. 26,* 221-5.

Hibbert, K.A. (1971) Teachers' attitudes towards psychologists. *Journal
of the Association of Educational Psychologists.* 2 (10), 25-32.

de Hirsch, K., Jansky, J.J. and Langford, W.S. (1967) *Predicting
Reading Failure.* New York: Harper and Row.

Howarth, C.I. (1975) The uses of psychology. In: W.E.C. Gillham (ed.)
Psychology Today. London: Hodder and Stoughton/Teach Yourself
Books.

Howells, J.G. (1974) *Remember Maria.* London: Butterworths.

Hutton, G. (1976) Environment, cohesion and differentiation in a
secondary school. In: E. Miller (ed.) *Task and Organization.* New
York: John Wiley.

Hunt, J. McV. (1961) *Intelligence and Experience.* New York: Ronald
Press.

Illich, I. (1973) *Deschooling Society.* London: Calder and Boyars.

Illich, I. (1975) *Medical Nemesis.* London: Calder and Boyars.

Immegart, G.L. and Pilecki, F.J. (1973) *An Introduction to Systems
for the Educational Administrator.* Reading, Mass: Addison-Wesley.

Ingleby, D. (1972) Ideology and the human sciences: some comments
on the role of reification in psychology and psychiatry. In: T.
Pateman (ed.) *Counter Course.* Harmondsworth: Penguin Books.

Iscoe, I. (1974) Community psychology and the competent community.
American Psychologist. 30, 607-13.

Jacobsen, E. (1938) *Progressive Relaxation.* Chicago: University of
Chicago Press.

Jansky, J.J. and de Hirsch, K. (1971) *Preventing Reading Failure.* New
York: Harper and Row.

Jenkins, G.M. (1972) The systems approach. In: J. Beishon and G.
Peters (eds) *Systems Behaviour.* London: Harper and Row for the
Open University.

Jensen, A.R. (1964) The Rorschach technique: a re-evaluation. *Acta*

Psychologica. 22, 60-77.

Kagan, J. (1971) *Understanding Children.* New York: Harcourt Brace Jovanovich.

Karnes, M.B. (1968) *Helping Young Children Develop Language Skills.* Arlington, Va.: The Council for Exceptional Children.

Kaye, K. (1973) IQ: a conceptual deterrent to revolution in education. *Elementary School Journal. 74,* 9-23.

Keir, G. (1952) A history of child guidance. *British Journal of Educational Psychology. 22,* 12-29.

Kirk, S.A. and Kirk, W.D. (1971) *Psycholinguistic Learning Disabilities.* Urbana, Ill.: University of Illinois Press.

Kirman, B.H. (1965) The educationally subnormal child. In: L.T. Hilliard and B.H. Kirman (eds) *Mental Deficiency.* (2nd edition). London: Churchill.

Kohlberg, L. (1963) Moral development and identification. In: H.W. Stevenson (ed.) *Child Psychology.* Chicago: University of Chicago Press.

Krumboltz, D. and Thorsen, C.E. (eds) (1969) *Behavioral Counseling: Cases and Techniques.* New York: Holt, Rinehart and Winston.

Labon, D. (1973) Some effects of school-based therapy. *Journal of the Association of Educational Psychologists. 3* (6), 28-34.

Latané, B. and Darley, J.M. (1968) Group inhibition of by-stander intervention in emergencies. *Journal of Personality and Social Psychology. 10,* 215-21.

Leach, D.J. and Raybould, E.C. (1977) *Learning and Behaviour Difficulties in School.* London: Open Books.

Lemert, E.M. (1962) Paranoia and the dynamics of exclusion. *Sociometry. 25,* 2-20. Reprinted in: E. Rubington and M.S. Weinberg (eds) *Deviance: The Interactionist Perspective.* New York: Macmillan (1968).

Levitt, E.E. (1971) Research on psychotherapy with children. In: A.E. Bergin and S.L. Garfield (eds) *Handbook of Psychotherapy and Behaviour Change.* London: John Wiley.

Lifton, R.J. (1961) *Thought Reform and the Psychology of Totalism.* London: Gollancz.

Lindsay, G.A. (1977) Monitoring children's progress and the early identification of learning difficulties. Unpublished interim research report: Sheffield Educational Department Psychological Service.

Liverant, S. (1960) Intelligence: a concept in need of re-examination. *Journal of Consulting Psychology. 24* (2), 101-10.

Loxley, D. (1974) Beyond child guidance. Paper presented to the

Northern Branch of the DECP.

Loxley, D. (1976) Redefining educational psychology: an alternative perspective. Unpublished paper: Sheffield Education Department Psychological Service.

Loxley, D. (1976) Community psychology: an alternative perspective. Unpublished paper: Sheffield Education Department Psychological Service.

Mager, R.F. (1972) *Goal Analysis*. San Francisco: Fearon Publications Inc.

Mager, R.F. (1975) *Preparing Instructional Objectives*. San Francisco: Fearon Publications Inc.

Maliphant, R. (1974) Educational psychology: testing, testing? (or will it be fine tomorrow). *Bulletin of the British Psychological Society.* 27, 441-7.

Matza, D. (1969) *Becoming Deviant.* New York: Prentice-Hall.

McClelland, D.C. (1973) Testing for competence rather than for intelligence. *American Psychologist. 28,* 1-14.

Mercer, J.R. (1973) *Labelling the Mentally Retarded.* Santa Barbara, Calif.: University of California Press.

Midwinter, E. (1977) The professional-lay relationship: a Victorian legacy. *Journal of Child Psychology and Child Psychiatry. 18* (2), 101-113.

Miller, E. (ed.) (1976) *Task and Organization.* New York: John Wiley.

Miller, P. (1973) All children are special. *Journal of the Association of Educational Psychologists. 3* (3), 40-46.

Ministry of Education (1955) *Report of the Committee on Maladjusted Children.* (Underwood Report). London: HMSO.

Mischel, W. (1968) *Personality and Assessment.* New York: John Wiley.

Mittler, P. (1973) Purposes and principles of assessment. In: P. Mittler (ed.) *Assessment for Learning in the Mentally Handicapped.* Edinburgh and London: Churchill Livingstone.

Montenegro, H. (1968) Severe psychotic anxiety in two preschool children successfully treated by reciprocal inhibition. *Journal of Child Psychology and Child Psychiatry. 9,* 93-103.

Moore, R.B.W. (1969) The nature of educational psychology in School Psychology and Child Guidance Services. *Bulletin of the British Psychological Society. 22,* 185-9.

Morgan, G. (1977) Integration versus segregation in Ontario. *Special Education. 4* (1), 18-21.

Morgan, J.H. (1971) DIY at Dinsdale Park School. *Special Education. 60* (4), 21-3.

Moseley, D. (1975) *Special Provision for Reading: When Will They Ever Learn?* Windsor: NFER.

Neisser, U. (1976) *Cognition and Reality.* San Francisco: W.H. Freeman.

Olson, D.F. (1975) The languages of experience: a natural language and formal education. *Bulletin of the British Psychological Society. 28,* 363-73.

Osgood, C.E. (1957) A behavioristic analysis. In: *Contemporary Approaches to Cognition.* Cambridge, Mass.: Harvard University Press.

Patterson, B.R.,McNeal, S., Hawkins, N. and Phelps, R. (1967) Reprogramming the social environment. *Journal of Child Psychology and Child Psychiatry. 8,* 181-95.

Phillips, C.J. (1971) Summerfield and after: the training of educational psychologists. *Bulletin of the British Psychological Society. 24,* 207-13.

Piaget, J. (1932) *The Moral Judgement of the Child.* London: Routledge and Kegan Paul.

Piaget, J. (1971) *Science of Education and the Psychology of the Child.* London, Longman.

Pidgeon, D.A. and Yates, A. (1956) The relationship between ability and attainment – an examination of current thory. *Bulletin of the NFER.* No. 8 (Nov. 1956), 24-8.

Pinchbeck, I. and Hewitt, M. (1973) *Children in English Society.* (Volume 2). London: Routledge and Kegan Paul.

Power, M.J., Benn, R.T. and Morris, J.N. (1967) Delinquent schools? *New Society.* 19 Oct. 1967.

Power, M.J., Benn, R.T. and Morris, J.N. (1972) Neighbourhood, school and juveniles before the courts. *British Journal of Criminology.* April, 111-32.

Presland, J. (1970) Who should go to ESN schools? *Special Education. 59* (1), 11-16.

Presland, J. (1970) Applied psychology and backwardness in handwriting. *Supplement to the Journal of the Association of Educational Psychologists. 2* (7).

Presland, J. (1973) Dealing with disturbing behaviour in the classroom. *Journal of the Association of Educational Psychologists. 3* (3), 28-32.

Presland, J. (1975) Advising on school behaviour modification. *Journal of the Association of Educational Psychologists. 3* (9), 5-9.

Preston, K. and Lindsay, G. (1976) Schoolgirl mothers. *New Society.*

14 Oct. 1967.

Pringle, M.K. (1974) *The Needs of Children.* London: Hutchinson.

Pritchard, D.G. (1963) *Education and the Handicapped: 1760-1960.* London: Routledge and Kegan Paul.

Rabinowitz, A. (1977) Discussion paper: children and their difficulties in school. Unpublished manuscript.

Ravenette, A.T. (1972) Maladjustment. Clinical concept and administrative convenience. Psychologists, teachers and children: how many ways to understand? *Journal of the Association of Educational Psychologists. 3* (2), 41-7.

Rehin, G. (1972) Child guidance at the end of the road. *Social Work Today. 2* (4), 21-4.

Reynolds, D. (1976) When pupils and teachers refuse a truce: the secondary school and the creation of delinquency. In: G. Mungham and G. Person (eds) *Working Class Youth Culture.* London: Routledge and Kegan Paul.

Reynolds, D. (1977) The delinquent school. In: M. Hammersley and P. Woods (eds) *The Process of Schooling.* London: Routledge and Kegan Paul.

Richman, N., Stevenson, J.E. and Graham, P.J. (1975) Prevalence of behaviour problems in three-year-old children: an epidemiological study in a London Borough. *Journal of Child Psychology and Child Psychiatry. 16* (4), 277-87.

Riegel, K.F. and Riegel, R.M. (1972) Development, drop and death. *Developmental Psychology. 6,* 306-19.

Robb, B. (ed.) (1967) *Sans Everything: A Case to Answer.* London: Nelson.

Robins, L.N. (1966) *Deviant Children Grown Up.* Baltimore: Williams and Wilkins.

Robins, L.N. (1970) Follow-up studies investigating childhood disorders. In: E.H. Hare and J.K. Wing (eds) *Psychiatric Epidemiology.* London: Oxford University Press.

Robins, L.N. (1972) Chapter in: H.C. Quay and J.S. Werry (eds) *Psychopathological Disorders of Childhood.* London: John Wiley.

Roe, A.M. (1975) Educational psychology: the view from the gun-deck. *Bulletin of the British Psychological Society. 28,* 199-200.

Rogers, C.R. (1951) *Client-centred Therapy.* New York: Houghton Mifflin.

Rosenthal, R. (1966) *Experimenter Effects in Behavioral Research.* New York: Appleton-Century-Crofts.

Rubington, E. and Weinberg, M.S. (eds) (1968) *Deviance: The Interactionist Perspective.* New York: Macmillan.

Rutter, M. (1965) Classification and categorization in child psychiatry.

Journal of Child Psychology and Child Psychiatry. 6, 71-83.

Rutter, M. (1975) *Helping Troubled Children.* Harmondsworth: Penguin Books.

Rutter, M., Cox, A., Dupling, C., Berger, M. and Yule, W. (1975) Attainment and adjustment in two geographical areas. *British Journal of Psychiatry. 126,* 493-519.

Rutter, M., Tizard, J. and Whitmore, K. (1970) *Education, Health and Behaviour.* London: Longman.

Sampson, O. (1975) A dream that is dying? *Bulletin of the British Psychological Society. 28,* 380-82.

Schaie, K.W. (1974) Translations in gerontology — from lab to life. *American Psychologist. 30,* 802-7.

Schubert, J. (1973) *Manual to the VRB apparatus.* University of Saskatchewan.

Schur, E.M. (1973) *Radical Non-intervention.* New York: Prentice-Hall.

Seligman, M.E.P. (1975) *Helplessness.* San Francisco: W.H. Freeman.

Shepherd, M., Oppenheim, B. and Mitchell, S. (1971) *Childhood Behaviour and Mental Health.* London: University of London Press.

Sheridan, M.D. (1962) Infants at risk of handicapping conditions. *Monthly Bulletin of the Minstry of Health and the Public Health Laboratory Service. 21,* 238.

Simmons, J.L. (1969) *Deviants.* Santa Barbara, Calif.: Glendessary Press.

Simon, B. (1953) *Intelligence Testing and the Comprehensive School.* London: Lawrence and Wishart.

Smedslund, J. (1977) Piaget's psychology in practice. *British Journal of Educational Psychology. 47,* 1-6.

Staats, A. (1968) *Learning, Language and Cognition.* New York: Holt, Rinehart and Winston.

Stott, D.H.,Marston, N.C. and Neill, S.J. (1975) *Taxonomy of Behaviour Disturbance.* London: University of London Press.

Stuart, L. (1977) Clinical psychology in the community: the Thamesmead Project. Paper presented to the Workshop on Community Psychology, Institute of Psychiatry, London.

Stufflebeam, D.L. (1968) Toward a science of educational evaluation. *Educational Technology. 8* (14), 5-12.

Sutton, A. (1975) Crisis in British psychology? or: The party's over. *MOPP Discussion Paper No. 6.*

Sutton, A. (1976) Child psychology and local government. *Journal of the Association of Educational Psychologists. 4* (1), 9-14.

Sutton, A. (1977) Defects in defectology. *Times Educational Supple-*

ment. 13 May, p. 46.

Sutton, A. (1977) Confidentiality: the professionals' dilemma. Unpublished ms.

Sutton, A. (1977) Advocacy. *Journal of the Association of Educational Psychologists. 4* (5), 12-15

Sutton, A. (1977) *The Developmental Psychology of L.S. Vygotskii.* (in preparation).

Szasz, T.S. (1961) *The Myth of Mental Illness.* New York: Harper and Row.

Tajfel, H. (1973) The roots of prejudice: cognitive aspects. In: P. Watson (ed.) *Psychology and Race.* Harmondsworth: Penguin Books.

Tannenbaum, F. (1938) *Crime and the Community.* New York: Columbia University Press.

Terman, L.M. (1917) *The Stanford Revision and Extension of the Binet-Simon Scale for Measuring Intelligence.* Baltimore: Warwick and York Inc.

Tizard, J. (1966) Schooling for the handicapped. *Special Education. 55* (2), 4-7.

Tizard, J. (1973) Maladjusted children and the child guidance service. *London Educational Review. 2* (2), 22-37.

Tizard, J. (1976) Psychology and social policy. *Bulletin of the British Psychological Society. 29,* 225-34.

Topping, K. (1977) Critical circular 'discovered'. *Journal of the Association of Educational Psychologists. 4* (4), 33-4.

Truax, C.B. and Carkhuff, R.R. (1968) *Toward Effective Counseling and Psychotherapy.* Chicago: Aldine.

Tuckman, B.W. (1975) *Measuring Educational Outcomes.* New York: Harcourt Brace Jovanovich.

Valentine, C.W. (1956) *The Normal Child – and some of his Abnormalities.* Harmondsworth: Penguin Books.

Vernon, P.E. (1958) A new look at intelligence testing. *Educational Research. 1,* 3-12.

Vernon, P.E. (1960) *Intelligence and Attainment Tests.* London: University of London Press.

Vernon, P.E. (1964) *Personality Assessment: A Critical Survey.* London: Methuen.

Vernon, P.E. (1968) What is potential ability? *Bulletin of the British Psychological Society. 21* (73), 211-19.

Vygotskii, L.S. (1956) *Selected Psychological Investigations.* (in Russian) Moscow: Academy of Pedagogic Sciences.

Vygotskii, L.S. (1960) *The Development of Higher Mental Functions.*

(in Russian) Moscow: Academy of Pedagogic Sciences.

Wall, W.D. (1955) *Education and Mental Health.* Paris: UNESCO.

Waller, W. (1932) *The Sociology of Teaching.* New York: John Wiley.

Ward, J. (1975) The current status of psychometry. *British Psychological Society DECP Occasional Papers.* 8, 380-87.

Ward, J. and Stratford, R. (1975) Preparing educational psychologists for an advisory role. *Journal of the Association of Educational Psychologists.* 3 (8), 19-23.

Wedell, K. (1973) *Learning and Perceptuo-motor Disabilities in Children.* London: John Wiley.

Weeks, E.J. (1966) Educational psychology and comprehensive schools. *Journal of the Association of Educational Psychologists.* 7, 6-9.

Werthman, C. (1963) Delinquents in school. In: B. Coslin *et al.* (eds) *School and Society.* London: Routledge and Kegan Paul for the Open University.

Whitmore, T.K. (1972) Maladjusted children. *Supplement to the Journal of the Association of Educational Psychologists.* 2 (7).

Wickman, E.K. (1928) *Children's Behavior and Teachers' Attitudes.* New York: Commonwealth Fund.

Williams, P. (1964) Date of birth, backwardness and educational organisation. *British Journal of Educational Psychology.* 34 (3), 247-55.

Williams, P. (1965) Ascertainment of educationally subnormal children. *Educational Research.* 7 (2), 136-46.

Williams, P. (1974) The growth and scope of the School Psychological Service. In: M. Chazan, T. Moore, P. Williams and H.J. Wright (eds) *The Practice of Educational Psychology.* London: Longman.

Williams, P. and Gruber, E. (1967) *Response to Special Schooling.* London: Longman.

Wolfendale, S. (1976) Working with teachers. *Journal of the Association of Educational Psychologists.* 4 (2), 20-24.

Wolfendale, S. (1976) Screening and early identification of reading and learning difficulties: a description of the Croydon screening procedures. In: K. Wedell and E.C. Raybould (eds) *The Early Identification of Educationally 'at-risk' Children.* University of Birmingham: Educational Review (Occasional publications No. 6).

Wolpe, J. (1973) *The Practice of Behavior Therapy.* (2nd edition) New York: Pergamon Press.

Woods, M. (1973) Caught in the act. *Journal of the Association of Educational Psychologists.* 3 (3), 32-6.

Wright, H.J. (1974) Relationships with colleagues. In: M. Chazan, T. Moore, P. Williams and H.J. Wright (eds) *The Practice of Educa-*

tional Psychology. London: Longman.

Wright, H.J. (1976) The practice of educational psychology in England and Wales as affected by recent changes in the Health Services and Local Government. *Journal of the Association of Educational Psychologists. 4* (2), 24-31.

CONTRIBUTORS

Robert Burden Tutor to the MEd course in Educational Psychology, University of Exeter.

Frank Carter Senior Educational Psychologist, Nottinghamshire School Psychological Service.

Tony Dessent Educational Psychologist, Cambridgeshire School Psychological Service.

Bill Gillham Tutor to the MA course in Child and Educational Psychology, University of Nottingham

David Hargreaves Reader in Education, University of Manchester.

Gervase Leyden Senior Educational Psychologist, Nottinghamshire School Psychological Service.

David Loxley Principal Psychologist, Sheffield Education Department Psychological Service.

Michael Roe Principal Educational Psychologist, London Borough of Bexley School Psychological Service.

Andrew Sutton Senior Educational Psychologist, Birmingham School Psychological Service and part-time lecturer, University of Birmingham.

INDEX